CANBY PUBLIC LIBRARY
292 N. HOLLY
CANBY, OR 97013

ANFN

P9-DUR-879

Greek and Roman Life

IAN JENKINS

ANNIAE
ARESCVSA

HARVARD UNIVERSITY PRESS

Cambridge, Massachusetts

1986

Copyright © 1986 by the Trustees of the British Museum
ISBN 0-674-36307-8

Library of Congress Catalog Card Number 86-80483

Reprinted 1987, 1990

Printed in Italy

THE TRUSTEES OF THE BRITISH MUSEUM acknowledge with gratitude the generosity of THE HENRY MOORE FOUNDATION for the grant which made possible the publication of this book.

Front cover Two terracotta models, showing a woman grinding grain and another baking bread. Greek, 5th century BC.

Inside front cover Writing implements: (back row) four leaves of a wooden writing tablet from Roman Egypt; Roman inkpots in faience, pottery and bronze, 1st and 2nd century AD; (front row) a letter written in Greek on papyrus, from Alexandria, 1st century AD; a reed pen from Roman Egypt; a Roman bronze pen; an ivory *stylus* for incising characters into the waxed surface of a writing tablet – the blunt end is for rubbing out (probably Greek); and a bronze *stylus* (probably Roman).

Title page Terracotta relief showing a chariot race. A four-horsed chariot approaches the three decorative columns of the turning-post. A *jubilator*, a rider who encourages the contestants, has already turned, while a charioteer reins in his team. A fallen charioteer crouches at the foot of the turning-post. Roman, made in Italy in the 1st century AD.

This page Newly arrived at her husband's home, a bride is led by him towards an altar. The couple are accompanied by a pipe-player and women holding blazing torches. At the altar stands a woman with a sceptre in her left hand and a sacrificial object in her right. She is perhaps a personification of Hestia, goddess of the hearth and home. Through her participation in a sacrifice at the altar, the bride will be placed under the protection of the household gods and so accepted as a new member of her husband's family. Scene from a white-ground *pyxis* (toilet box) made in Athens c.470–460 BC and attributed to the Splanchnopt Painter.

Inside back cover Wall-painting from the Garden Room of the Villa of Livia at Prima Porta. Reign of Augustus (27 BC–AD 14). Rome, Museo Nazionale delle Terme.

Back cover Silver statuette of a shepherd carrying a sheep in a bag slung over his shoulder. Roman, probably 1st century AD.

Contents

Preface *page* 4

1 The Home 5

2 The Family and the Role of Women 15

3 Dress 23

4 Children and Education 30

5 Marriage and Death 38

6 Greek Athletic and Dramatic Festivals 44

7 Roman Games and Gladiators 55

8 Work and Slavery 62

Further reading 71

Passages quoted 71

Photo acknowledgements 71

List of registration and catalogue numbers 71

Index 72

Preface

This book is intended to accompany the British Museum's exhibition of Greek and Roman daily life, providing a background to some of the topics illustrated there.

There are many advantages in exhibiting Greek and Roman culture side by side. The two may be compared with a view to bringing out the similarities and the differences. What is said, however, of the Greeks will not always apply to the Romans, and vice-versa. In order to avoid confusion, therefore, every effort has been made to clarify whether a statement is true of the Greeks or of the Romans, or both. Sometimes the distinction is drawn even more finely, as, for example, between what must be considered a specifically Athenian custom and one which may be regarded more widely as Greek. For although we write and speak freely of 'the Greeks' and 'the Romans', many of our generalisations derive all too often from particular sources. If fifth-century Athens and late Republican and early Imperial Rome loom large in the following pages, it is because our main body of evidence comes from these places and these periods.

The exhibition illustrates Greek and Roman private and public life, and the scope of this book is equally wide-ranging. It would be impossible, however, to give a comprehensive account in so short a space. Not every topic has been treated in equal depth, and some have been omitted altogether. Little, for example, is said of the army and war, on which there are a number of good popular and specialist books. The same is true of government and law, which are not, in fact, featured in the exhibition, since they are not easily illustrated through the collections of the British Museum.

This book focuses on life in the home, which in antiquity was the nucleus of all social, economic and, indeed, political activity. By concentrating on the domestic lives of people, we see a different side of Classical antiquity from that which is presented through the more traditional forms of political and military history.

I have received invaluable assistance from a number of friends and colleagues during the preparation of this book, and I should like to thank the following for reading drafts of the text and for making many helpful comments: Donald Bailey, Lucilla Burn, Brian Cook, Lesley Fitton, Teresa Francis, Christopher Lightfoot, Patsy Vanags, Andrew Wallace-Hadrill, Dyfri Williams and Susan Woodford. I must also thank Sue Bird for preparing the line drawings and Jim Hendry and Ivor Kerslake for taking the photographs. Finally, special thanks are due to Frances Dunkels.

FOR MY PARENTS

Ian Jenkins
June 1985

1 The Home

'An Englishman's home is his castle', as the saying goes, but this was probably even more true of the ancient Greeks and Romans. Both peoples were deeply conscious of the boundaries, social as well as physical, that divided public from private life. Most houses, Greek as well as Roman, large and small, town and country, were built to an inward-looking design with rooms arranged around a central courtyard, the chief considerations being privacy and security.

Throughout Classical antiquity houses were built mostly of brick, which was cheap and easy to manufacture and use. Solid masonry was costly and difficult to work, and was therefore usually reserved for civic and religious buildings. The Romans made good use of their distinctive kiln-fired brickwork, not only in domestic buildings but also in public works on a larger scale. Commonly, however, and particularly in Greece, houses were built simply out of sun-dried mud-brick, reinforced perhaps with timbers, supported on stone foundations. Mud-brick is not a durable material and rapidly decomposes. All too often, therefore, in attempting to reconstruct an ancient house the archaeologist is faced with scanty or uncertain evidence. Usually nothing survives above ground and perhaps the only indication of where a building once stood is a murky outline staining the earth. Scattered debris may indicate how the walls were constructed and the roof covered. Anything that could be salvaged from the house, however, is likely to have been removed in antiquity. Stone foundations, for example, are liable to have been robbed and used elsewhere. The Greek historian Thucydides relates how, towards the end of the fifth century BC, country-dwelling Athenians were forced by the war with Sparta to leave their homes. They sought refuge within the city walls and, we are told, took their wooden doors and shutters with them. Wood was scarce in Attica, and these were a portable, re-usable commodity. Thus, for those whose homes would never be re-occupied, the process of dismantlement had already begun; nature and time would take care of the rest.

The Roman House

The archaeological record tells us less about Greek houses than Roman ones, which give us the best insight into domestic arrangements in Classical times. There are few destructive forces more devastating than gradual erosion. For the archaeologist, therefore, it is better that a site should have been destroyed suddenly by earthquake, fire or, best of all, volcanic eruption. Nowhere are the archaeological advantages of the latter demonstrated more dramatically than in the Roman towns of Pompeii and Herculaneum. Here, within the space of a few hours on 24 August AD 79, the volcanic discharge from Mount Vesuvius buried town and country for miles around. The event can be accurately dated because of a

1 Reconstruction of a *domus*-type house.

5

letter written by the younger Pliny to the Roman historian Tacitus in which it is graphically described. Pliny relates how the panic-stricken people fled their houses and villas, leaving not only their homes but in many cases their personal belongings as well. They never returned and it was not until the eighteenth century that Pompeii and Herculaneum were rediscovered. The process of excavating and restoring the extensive and remarkably well-preserved remains continues to this day.

At Pompeii by AD 79, as in any town with a history, there were older and newer houses standing side by side. In many cases it is possible to see how, as the years went by, the nucleus of an older-style dwelling was adapted and expanded. Some Pompeian houses evacuated in AD 79 still retained the fabric of the original house built centuries before. Such, for example, was the sturdy so-called House of Sallust, built of limestone during the late fourth or early third century BC. Although by the time of the eruption the internal arrangement was somewhat altered, it is nevertheless possible to visualise how the house originally looked. In his treatise on architecture, written around 25 BC, Vitruvius refers to this type of house by the word *domus*. The old-style *domus* consisted of a central hall known as an *atrium*, with rooms – each with their separate function – grouped around. At some point during the second century BC the roof of the atrium in the House of Sallust was fitted with a skylight, or *compluvium*. As well as light, this rectangular opening admitted rainwater, which ran off the inward-sloping roof and fell into a sunken basin or *impluvium*. From here water drained through a pipe to a cistern at the back of the house, from which the family drew its daily supply.

In the atrium we might expect to find the household shrine or *lararium*. Here were kept figures representing the household gods, the *lares* and the *penates*. The atrium would also

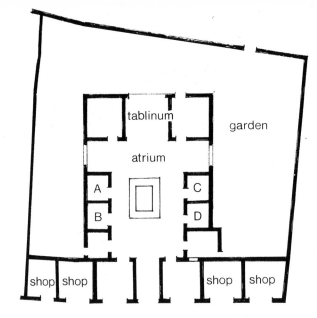

ABCD – bedrooms

have contained the family strong-box. It was entered from the street through a porch (*vestibulum*) and a short passage which lay beyond. (By the second century BC the front of the House of Sallust had been adapted to accommodate a line of shops.) Bedrooms (*cubicula*) flanked the atrium, and beyond them two *alae* (wings) gave access to three larger rooms. In the middle of these was the *tablinum*. In earliest days this is thought to have served as a master-bedroom, and the family archives are also said to have been kept in here. Formal dinners, it seems, were originally held in the atrium, but by the second century BC one of the two rooms on either side of the *tablinum* in the House of Sallust was being used as a dining room, or *triclinium*. The name derives from the Greek word for a dining-couch (*klinē*), and it seems the Romans acquired from the Greeks the habit of reclining to eat, usually with three couches arranged around the walls of a room.

The traditional *domus* satisfied in every respect the dual requirements of privacy and

2 Plan of the House of Sallust in the 2nd century BC.

3 (*right, above*) A *lararium* in the House of the Vettii, Pompeii, with painted representations of household gods: in the middle, the *genius* holding a libation bowl and a box of offerings; on either side of him the *lares*, each with a drinking horn and a ritual bucket; below, a snake about to take an offering from an altar.

4 Household gods: a *lar* holds a drinking horn in his right hand and a bowl for pouring ritual libations in his left; a *genius* shown with head veiled in the manner of a priest performing sacrifice; one of the *penates*, protective spirits associated in particular with the larder, holding a cornucopia and libation bowl; and a bearded snake. Roman, probably all 1st century AD.

security. The atmosphere inside was perhaps a little gloomy as a result. Here the head of the Roman household, the *paterfamilias*, held sway over his private domain. Here he jealously guarded the power of life and death he possessed over the family and household slaves under his protection. Yet the austere apartments of the *domus* were not entirely closed to the outside world. The house, and in particular the *tablinum*, lay at the centre of a network of social relations that bridged the gap between public and private life. Throughout Roman history it was the custom for free but poor citizens to place themselves under the protection of a wealthy and politically powerful patron. In return for daily handouts and the promise of legal aid, the *clientes*, as they were known, pledged their loyalty and support. They performed a daily ritual of *salutatio*, greeting their patron every morning. We can picture them making their way through the dark entrance to the atrium, perhaps pausing here to await their turn for interview. In the *tablinum* the *patronus* heard their pleas and dictated his own desires. Although open to the atrium, the *tablinum* could be closed off and made private by means of a portable screen such as that found in the so-called House of the Wooden Partition at Herculaneum. After consultation the *clientes* retraced their steps and re-emerged into the light of day, going forth as ambassadors for their patron's good name in the world outside. It is probably the *clientes* Vitruvius has in mind when he says, 'Men of ordinary fortune do not need entrance-halls, *tablina* or an atrium built in the grand style, because such men are more inclined to discharge their social obligation by going round to others than by having others come to them.'

The House of Sallust serves as an example of the traditional type of dwelling which would have been inhabited by well-to-do families living in Italy down to the end of the third century BC. After this period we can detect a number of changes taking place in the traditional house design. These are directly linked to the political history of Rome and reflect new cultural ideas coming to Italy from Rome's growing empire, in particular from Greece.

The Greek east was rich, both in substance and in culture. The eastward expansion of Rome's political and commercial interests meant that there was both more money in Republican Rome and more to spend it on. Contemporary conservative opinion cried out against a tendency to luxury, which was considered to be eating away at the traditionally self-contained character and customs of the Roman people.

The impact of Greek cultural influence was felt not least in the harbour towns on the Bay of Naples. Its effect can be seen clearly in the houses of Pompeii. For example, during the second century BC the prosperous owner of the so-called House of Pansa decided to embellish his traditional *domus* by extending it over the garden at the back. In keeping with a new interest in Greek domestic architecture the extension featured a large colonnade surrounding an ornamental pool. The courtyard was of central importance to Greek family life. Here behind a high surrounding wall the household was able to conduct its daily routine safe from the eyes of prying strangers, while at the same time enjoying the benefits of the Mediterranean climate. In the extension to the House of Pansa, the colonnaded court is borrowed as an architectural feature but, as so often in architectural borrowing, it loses its former function and takes on a new, more decorative role. Fitted with a pool or planted with a garden, the colonnaded court now became a place for rest and recreation and for the exhibition of sculpture.

A garden had already been a feature of the old-style *domus*, where it was enclosed by a wall. But gardening for pleasure on any scale seems to have been another import from

ABCDEF — bedrooms

5 Plan of the House of Pansa in the 2nd century BC. The shaded area indicates the extent of the original house. After McKay.

6 Two views of the interior of a sarcophagus carved with an effigy of the deceased, surrounded by the personal belongings and amenities she would need in the afterlife. Roman, probably early 2nd century AD. Leiden, National Museum of Antiquities.

7 A view of the garden belonging to the House of M. Loreius Tiburtinus, Pompeii.

Hellenistic Greece. One of the most magnificent gardens to come to light at Pompeii is that belonging to the house of Marcus Loreius Tiburtinus, which was divided into two by a water channel fed by a fountain. Archaeologists who found root cavities preserved in the volcanic soil were able to identify fruit trees and bushes that once grew here and have replanted the garden accordingly.

The garden and its surrounding colonnade (peristyle) brought a new point of focus to the *domus*. The House of Loreius Tiburtinus, for example, was fitted with a summer dining-room looking out from the terrace over the

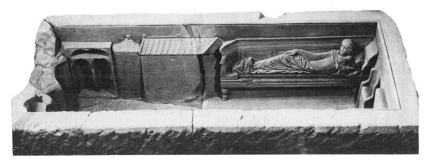

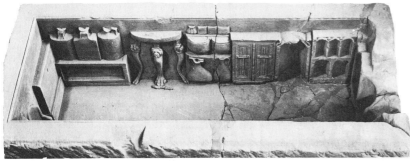

garden beyond. As interest shifted to the lighter, more airy regions of the house around the peristyle, in summer at least the atrium must have lost some of its former prestige as the physical and social centre of the home. It was far from superseded, however, and remained a dominant feature in Pompeian houses down to AD 79. Yet the effects of Hellenism may be seen at work, even in this hallowed quarter. The old *impluvia*, for example, had been made of terracotta or the local volcanic limestone. These were now often replaced with more fashionable marble versions. Again, to demonstrate the householder's enthusiasm for current trends, real or imitation marble columns were introduced into the atrium.

One of the most colourful developments in Pompeian interiors from the second century BC onwards was the introduction of wall-painting. The first phase of Pompeian wall-painting used artificial marbling, which appears to have been popular in widespread regions of the Greek east from the fourth century BC onwards. In the House of Sallust stucco was applied to the wall in a kind of low relief and imitation marble painted over it. When we come to the first century BC we find a new, more elaborate conception of wall-decoration. At first the idea of simulated marble panelling is kept, but from around 80 BC onwards columns also appear, painted as though they stand free of the wall. This tendency to create 8 the illusion of receding depth continues until the upper half of the wall is, as it were, cut away to provide a view through the wall into a fantasy world beyond. In addition to these two phases of wall-painting, two further 'styles' can be identified before the development of this most attractive feature of Pompeian interior decoration was brought to an abrupt end by the disaster of AD 79.

We have lingered in the houses of Pompeii because it is here that we gain our fullest

8 (*left*) Second-style wall-painting in the Villa of the Mysteries, Pompeii. 1st century BC.

9 Restored frontage of an *insula* at Ostia in the 2nd century AD, with apartments on the upper floors and shops below. After Boëthius and Ward-Perkins.

knowledge of Roman domestic architecture. It would be a mistake, however, to assume that every Roman enjoyed the splendour of these surroundings. In Rome, for example, most people inhabited a very different sort of dwelling. At Ostia, the harbour town of the capital city, there survive substantial remains of the kind of tenement-block, or *insula*, for which Rome itself was notorious. The ever-increasing size of Rome's population from the third century BC onwards created a shortage of space. A remedy for urban overcrowding was sought in 'high-rise', a concept all too familiar in our own age. Indeed, it is the modern appearance of the Roman tenement-block that strikes the tourist at Ostia today.

The invention of concrete and the versatility of Roman brickwork enabled the building speculators of the ancient city to raise its population far above the ground. The higher they built, the more profitable the enterprise became for unprincipled landlords. The urban 'mob' lived cramped in rented apartments which frequently cost them their lives, either through the structure collapsing or from fire, which was an ever-present threat to all Romans. Naked flames in oil lamps and open braziers for heating added to the risk. Multi-storey buildings created yet further problems: while some ground-floor apartments enjoyed the benefits of piped water, those in the upper reaches of the tenements were obliged to employ the age-old method of fetch and carry, a chore which the multitude of stairs must have made all the more wearisome. Further, although Rome's impressive network of sewers – the Cloaca Maxima being the oldest and largest surviving example – bears testimony to the ingenuity of Roman engineering, nevertheless most Romans, and in particular those in high-rise apartments, were denied the benefit of domestic drainage. Even a cess-pit was out of the question for these last, and they were obliged to carry their sewage to the nearest disposal point. Frequently, it seems, this turned out to be no further than an open window. Many an outraged passer-by had recourse to the jury-courts to claim compensation against this unpleasant form of defenestration. As a more hygienic alternative, public sanitation was provided at the communal baths for which ancient Rome is famous and which were an important part of social life for rich and poor alike.

It is not surprising that those who could afford to do so sought refuge from the squalor and noise of Rome in their country villas. Increasingly in the last days of the Republic and during the Empire wealthy Romans built impressive mansions, many of which were in fact glorified farmhouses where the produce harvested by scores of slaves was stored and processed. The economic function of the villa was usually placed under the supervision of a bailiff, who would ensure the smooth and profitable running of the estate during the owner's absence. Fine domestic apartments, however, also provided the master and his family with a comfortable residence.

Other villas had a more ornamental role. The Romans were as fond of sea air as any leisured people, and the Bay of Naples became a particularly fashionable resort. The rich and the powerful vied with each other in the number and splendour of their seaside villas. Here the external anonymity which can usually be taken as the hallmark of Roman domestic architecture was abandoned in favour of elegant porticoes boasting to the seafaring world of the owner's taste and opulence. Under the Empire it was the emperor's privilege to outdo all in this game of one-upmanship, and the imperial palace underlined the great gulf that separated the humble apartments of the poor majority from the marbled halls of the wealthy few.

The Greek House
In Greece there is nothing to compare with the extensively preserved remains of Pompeii and Herculaneum. The nearest equivalent, perhaps, is the settlement at Akrotiri on the island of Santorini (ancient Thera), where archaeologists have uncovered considerable remains of houses buried in the Bronze Age by a volcanic explosion. This is an isolated instance, however, and our evidence for housing in the later period of Greek history is less spectacular and less complete. One of the better-preserved sites is that of Olynthos in northern Greece. Here a town laid out along the lines of a rectangular grid-plan was destroyed by the Macedonians in 348 BC. The townspeople lived, it seems, in small houses neatly arranged around a courtyard. Most of the rooms of the house looked onto the court, concealed from the street. It is interesting to remark upon

the frequency with which the excavators of Olynthos discovered an altar standing in the courtyard. Both Greek and Roman houses had an important religious dimension, with different gods protecting the different parts: the threshold, the courtyard and the store-rooms were all watched over by their respective deities, and at the notional centre of all family life was the sacred hearth.

Although the notoriously winding streets of Athens would not have allowed anything like the regular plan of Olynthian houses, nevertheless the same principle of rooms arranged around a central courtyard applied here, as can be seen in the few houses that have been excavated within the city walls. The houses of Athens in the fifth century BC are said to have been modest, and their appearance belied the great age in which their inhabitants lived. In contrast to the splendour of the city's public buildings with their elegant porticoed façades and ornate sculptures, domestic dwellings were unpretentious and not intended to draw the eye of the spectator.

In general we know more about the houses in the countryside, where the shallow remains of their foundations have not been disturbed by modern building. In a country district to

11 (right) Wall-painting from Stabiae, showing a villa by the sea. Roman, 1st century AD. Naples, Archaeological Museum.

10 A country house inhabited by a family living to the south of Athens around 350–300 BC. The inhabitants were farmers, and remains of stone-walled enclosures near the house suggest sheep-pens and places for growing crops and fruit trees. Bees were also kept, in pottery hives of a type still used in parts of the Mediterranean today. The house was built of mud-brick on stone foundations. Stone flagging was laid over the surface of the courtyard, and the roof was protected by pottery tiles. The courtyard had a south-facing verandah, where the family could work or relax, shaded from the sun in summer and protected from winter winds. After Jones, Graham and Sackett.

the south of Athens, for example, near a place now known as Vari, archaeologists discovered a house inhabited by a farming family around 350–300 BC. The site commands fine views and the house was built on a promontory facing south, taking best advantage of the Mediterranean climate. In this remote part of Attica, far from the city, the house was particularly vulnerable to attack. There was hardly a time in the fifth century BC when Athens was not at war, either with Persia, in the early part of the century, or later with other Greeks, notably the Spartans. An additional threat might be caused by disputes between rival families, which were frequent in the ancient world and often led to bloody feuds. In the country, therefore, security was of paramount importance in house design. In the house at Vari the thickening of the foundations in one corner suggested to archaeologists that it had been equipped with a defensive tower. Such towers were commonplace in country houses and are mentioned in the ancient literary sources. A law-court speech by the orator Demosthenes recalls how, during a private dispute, the women of a certain household were obliged to take refuge in the tower when the opposing party had forced an entry into their home.

12 Terracotta model of a woman in a bath. The bath is only big enough to sit up in. It has a depression at the foot end for scooping up water, which was then thrown over the body. Greek, c.450 BC.

2 The Family and the Role of Women

In antiquity the family (Greek *oikos*, Roman *familia*) was patrilineal, that is to say the line of descent and the transfer of inheritance was from father to son. The principal male member of the household, whom the Romans called the *paterfamilias*, held sway over home and family. His wife would have a supervisory role in the house, but ultimate authority resided with him.

Under the rule (*manus*) of the *paterfamilias* and his Greek equivalent came both the female and the lesser male members of the household – sons, younger unmarried brothers, slaves and perhaps also his own father. The latter, having once been the head of the family, would in due course abdicate in favour of his younger, more powerful heir. The meaning of the words *familia* and *oikos*, moreover, embraced not only the human members of the household, but could also refer to its animals and inanimate property.

The family unit had a political as well as a domestic function. It was the 'patrician' families of Republican Rome who made up the ranks of the governing body, the Senate. Under the Empire the city was ruled by Rome's leading family, that of the emperor himself. Similarly, although by the fifth century BC Athens was constitutionally a democracy, nevertheless the government tended still to be dominated by a few leading families. This was true of most cities, whatever the form of government, throughout antiquity.

Such families were not necessarily made up of members residing under one roof, for inevitably each generation created new off-shoots as sons took their share of the family inheritance and went to live away from the parental home. These independent households were linked, however, by a bond of kinship and could combine to present a powerful political and even military force. Well-to-do Romans, in particular, reinforced family prestige, as we have already seen, through the system of client patronage. Moreover, if a slave acquired his freedom, he would adopt the name of his former master and so extend still further the sphere of that man's influence.

Ever since the nineteenth century, when scholars first became seriously interested in the social life of the ancients, there has been a debate over the status of women in ancient, and particularly Greek, society. Some have attempted to show that women were not unduly restricted; others insist that they lived in a state of near-oriental seclusion. This appears to be true at least for Classical Athens, but we have very little evidence of social practice in other parts of Greece. If any generalisation is possible, it may be said that in most parts of ancient Greece and the Roman Empire women did not enjoy anything like the freedom that a woman in Western Europe today might take for granted. It is difficult, however, to say what degree of freedom was given to women in any one place, at any one time. Nor do we know what women themselves thought of their lot. Such documentary sources as we have, reflect almost exclusively what men thought and wrote. This fact alone, perhaps, gives sufficient indication of the extent to which a woman's powers to express publicly or record an opinion were limited.

The only sphere of public activity in which women could aspire to office was religion, and a number of women from the ancient world are known to us solely because their names are recorded as priestesses of some cult. In all the other major civic activities – war, politics and law – women in both Greece and Rome were excluded by virtue of their sex. No one ever seriously suggested that women should have the vote, any more than that slaves had a right to be free. The political and social status of women and slaves was in many ways similar.

The exceptions often only go to prove the rule. In the theatre, for example, the powerful women of Greek tragedy held the fascination of the audience by behaving in a manner contrary to contemporary social custom. Such was Clytemnestra who, in Aeschylus's *Agamemnon*, ruled her house like a man during her husband's absence and then conspired with her lover to murder the king upon his return. Role reversal was a favourite theme in comedy, and the playwright Aristophanes frequently parodied the women of Athens by portraying them in situations that were normally the male preserve.

One notable, real-life exception was Aspasia. She was the consort of the famous Athenian statesman Pericles, and is said to have exerted a certain political influence when he led the Athenian democracy during the fifth century BC. Aspasia was a courtesan, however, and thereby exempt from the normal restrictions imposed upon the respectable wives of Athenian citizens. Moreover, the higher a woman's status in society, the less freedom she was likely to have. The Athenians looked down upon men who were forced by poverty to send their wives out to perform such menial tasks as keeping market stalls or wet-nursing. A woman who stayed at home preserved her pale complexion along with her virtue, and the former was prized as an indication of the latter.

Even inside the home the Athenian woman was not free to come and go as she pleased. She had her own quarters, the *gynaikonitis*, usually set at the back of the house and furthest away from the street. The Roman writer Cornelius Nepos remarks upon the fact of women's quarters in the Greek house and, still more puzzling to him, the attitude of Greek men towards their womenfolk:

Much that we hold to be correct in Rome is thought shocking in Greece. No Roman thinks it an embarrassment to take his wife to a dinner party. At home the wife [*materfamilias*] holds first place, and is the centre of its social life. Things are very different in Greece, where the wife is never present at dinner, unless it is a family party, and spends all her time in a remote part of the house called the Women's Quarter, which is never entered by the man unless he is a very close relative.

The opposite pole to the women's quarters was the *andron*. This was the room in which the men of the house entertained their guests. Many of the houses at Olynthos were equipped with an *andron*, often placed close to the entrance, just off the street. This meant that guests attending a drinking party (*symposium*) 13, 14 could do so without entering the inner parts of the house and so running the risk of confrontation with the host's female relatives. Athenian men were anxious almost to the point of neurosis, it seems, about the virtue of their own women. They thought nothing, however, of importing courtesans into the *andron* for the amusement of their guests. These female entertainers were known as *hetairai* ('companions'). Many were accomplished musicians and dancers, often having been reared to their profession from birth.

As the passage from Cornelius Nepos indicates, everyday life seems to have been somewhat less restricted for the Roman housewife. The Roman authors, moreover, have handed down to us some remarkable portraits of women who were clearly very accomplished. Cornelia, the daughter of Metellus Scipio, for example, was of free and noble birth. Her second husband was the general and statesman Pompey. This is how the historian Plutarch describes her:

The young woman had many charms apart from her youthful beauty. She was well versed in literature, in playing the lyre, and in geometry, and had been accustomed to listen to philosophical discourses with profit. In addition to this, she had a nature which was free from the unpleasant officiousness which such accomplishments are apt to impart to young women.

The author's tone is perhaps a little condes-

14 Greek drinking vessels:
(a) *psykter* (wine cooler);
(b) *stamnos* (storage jar);
(c) *amphora* (storage jar);
(d) *bell-krater* (bowl for mixing wine and water); (e) *column-krater* (bowl for mixing wine and water); (f) *kylix* (drinking cup) seen from below; (g) *kylix* (h) stemless *kylix*; (i) *skyphos* (drinking cup); (j) bronze wine strainer and 'dipper'; (k) small bowls for salt and titbits; (l) *oinochoai* (wine jugs). Greek, 5th century BC.

13 A youth and a bearded man recline on couches at a drinking party, accompanied by two women entertainers (*hetairai*). A third youth enters from the left, holding a musical instrument (*barbitos*). Scene from a red-figured *kylix* (drinking cup) made in Athens *c.*490–480 BC.

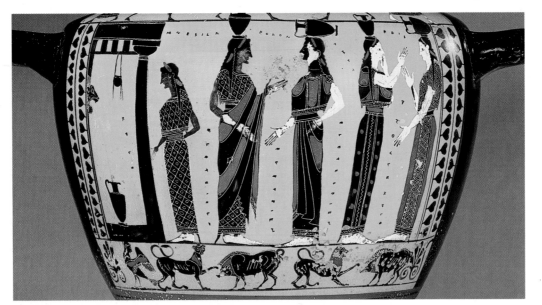

15 Women conversing at a fountain house. Two women are shown returning from the fountain with full jars carried upright on their heads, while two more approach with their vessels carried sideways. A fifth woman stands waiting for her jar to fill with water from the lion-headed spout. It is not clear whether the women are carrying out an everyday chore or whether the water is being fetched for a special occasion, such as a religious festival. Normally water-carrying would have been done only by poor women or slaves. Scene from a black-figured *hydria* (water jar) made in Athens *c*.520–500 BC.

16 Roman pots and pans: a bronze shell-shaped serving vessel; a bronze strainer; a terracotta mortar and pestle for grinding food (made by the potter Candidus, who worked near St Albans *c*.AD 95–135); a bronze saucepan with silvered interior; a bronze frying-pan, and a bronze baking pan. All *c*. 1st century AD.

cending, but it would be difficult to imagine an Athenian making the same observation about any woman of his acquaintance, other than a courtesan.

Female virtue, as reckoned by men, stood in direct proportion to how well a woman performed her work. In well-to-do households, no doubt, such tasks as fetching water and the 15–18 preparation of food were delegated to slaves, but in Greece even the aristocratic housewife was expected to participate in those most respected of household chores, namely spinning and weaving. Roman women also were commended for their skill in this respect, although it seems that in fashionable Roman society the wearing of homespun garments had become a thing of the past by the opening years of the first century AD. Augustus's insistence on setting the high-born women of the imperial household to the task of spinning and weaving his clothes was therefore curiously anachronistic. It was no doubt intended to demonstrate the emperor's approval of traditional Roman values, and in particular wifely virtues, which conservative opinion considered to have fallen into a decline.

Sadly, next to nothing has survived of the highly accomplished textile art which, from literary sources and pictorial representations, we know existed in ancient Greece and Rome. The Mediterranean climate, alternating between hot, dry summers and cold, wet winters, does not provide such ideal conditions for preservation as the dry sands of Egypt or the waterlogged peat of Scandinavia. A few scraps have, however, been recovered by archaeologists, and two of the most remarkable discoveries from Greece have been made in recent years. One of these, found at a site known as Lefkandi, on the island of Euboea, consisted of two sides of a linen tunic that had been rolled up and placed inside a bronze vessel. This had been deposited, together with other objects, in a shaft-grave dating to the tenth century BC.

17 (*right*) Pounding boiled and dried grain to make *pilgouri* (cracked wheat), at Karditsa, modern Greece.

18 Two women pounding grain in a mortar. From a black-figured *amphora* made in Athens *c.*540–520 BC. Leningrad, Hermitage.

From the fourth century BC come two trapezoidal pieces of cloth, woven in the form of a tapestry with gold and purple thread. These were found in the royal tomb at Vergina in Macedonia, northern Greece, thought by most scholars to be that of Philip II of Macedon, father of Alexander the Great. For the most part, however, the fruits of a labour that must have employed most of the waking hours of generations of Greek and Roman women are lost for ever.

Spinning and weaving were especially important in the home because this was one area where the family could achieve its ideal of economic self-sufficiency. Throughout antiquity wool was the commonest material used. Landowning families would furnish their own from the sheep reared on their estates, and the women of the household provided a ready source of cheap labour. Linen was the next most commonly used fabric. Most areas of mainland Greece and Italy, however, did not have sufficiently large tracts of fertile land for the growing of flax. Raw flax and linen were therefore imported from elsewhere. Other more fertile regions of the

19 (*above*) A group of instruments for spinning and weaving: a miniature pottery model of a *kalathos*, or wool basket (Greek, 6th century BC); a silver distaff and a wooden spindle (Roman, 1st century AD and Greek, 5th–4th century BC), and three spinning whorls (Greek, 6th–3rd century BC).

a   b   c   d   e

Mediterranean, such as Egypt, specialised in the production and export of this commodity. Another imported and especially luxurious fabric was silk. Even in Roman times, when the Empire penetrated deep into Asia and trade with China and India was relatively easy, silk remained a rare and expensive substance. Cotton, although widely grown in Greece today, was perhaps as rare or even rarer than silk. Herodotus, writing in the fifth century BC, is the first to mention it, as an exotic substance growing at the eastern edges of the earth. It was not, perhaps, until Alexander's armies conquered India that the Greeks first made use of cotton: Alexander's soldiers are said to have stuffed their saddles with cotton wool. The Romans certainly made use of it, notably for sails and for the awnings of open-air theatres.

Wool was therefore the material most readily available to the Greeks and Romans. A series of laborious tasks transformed it from the raw fibre to the finished textile. First, the fleece had to be cleaned to remove its country grease and grime, ready for dyeing. A variety of mineral and vegetable dyes were available to the ancients, but the colour most highly

prized was purple. True purple (there were a number of cheaper alternatives) was produced from the murex shellfish gathered along the coast of the eastern Mediterranean. Murex purple was valued for the brilliance and permanence of its colour.

After dyeing, the wool was spun by a method that can still be seen in parts of the Mediterranean world today. Neither the ancient Greeks nor the Romans had the use of the spinning wheel. Instead, a distaff and spindle were used in a simple method of hand-spinning. Endless hours were spent in the preparation of yarn, and women became expert spinners as a result. Poor women would earn a pittance by spinning for the market, and even courtesans, to judge from Athenian vase-paintings, ran a sideline in yarn.

Once the yarn was spun it was ready for weaving. The process of weaving, although apparently complicated, is based upon the simple principle of darning, one set of threads known as the weft crossing at right angles another set known as the warp. In the Classical world the warp was hung from the cross-bar of an upright loom. The lower end of the

20 Women working wool. Figures **a**, **b** and **f** prepare roves of wool for spinning (**a** is seated and wears a cloak over her *peplos*, perhaps here to indicate her rank as mistress of the household and supervisor of the work); **c** and **d** fold cloth and place it on the stool beside them; **e** spins with a distaff and spindle; **g** and **h** are weaving on a warp-weighted loom; **i** holds a pair of scales and, with the assistance of **j**, is weighing bales of wool; **k** is perhaps keeping count. Scene from a black-figured *lekythos* (oil flask) made in Athens around 540 BC and attributed to the Amasis Painter. New York, The Metropolitan Museum of Art.

21

22, 23

f   g   h   i   j   k

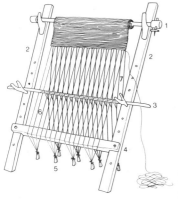

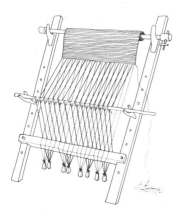

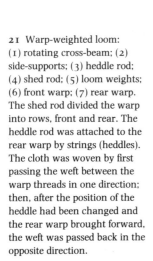

warp was then either secured to a second cross-bar, as we sometimes see it in Roman representations, or it was anchored with the use of loom-weights. The warp-weighted loom, as the latter type is known, appears to have been the most popular form in Greece. Its use was widespread among the peoples of ancient Europe, where it has a long history. In the 1950s a Norwegian scholar named Marta Hoffmann recorded the survival of warp-weighted looms among Lapp and Finnish weavers. Her descriptions and photographs are now invaluable in explaining the technical details of the ancient loom, which are only schematically rendered in Greek vase-painting.

The ancient loom was used to manufacture a variety of textiles needed in the home. There were, for example, the cushions and covers that were used to make wooden furniture both more attractive and more comfortable. In addition, hangings concealed bare walls and kept out winter draughts. It is often said of Greek houses that they were stark and sparsely furnished inside. We should always remember, however, to imagine the soft furnishings that must have contributed considerably to the atmosphere of the interior, and prosperous householders in particular would display their wealth to their guests through the textiles chosen to adorn the room.

21 Warp-weighted loom: (1) rotating cross-beam; (2) side-supports; (3) heddle rod; (4) shed rod; (5) loom weights; (6) front warp; (7) rear warp. The shed rod divided the warp into rows, front and rear. The heddle rod was attached to the rear warp by strings (heddles). The cloth was woven by first passing the weft between the warp threads in one direction; then, after the position of the heddle had been changed and the rear warp brought forward, the weft was passed back in the opposite direction.

22 (*left, above*) A woman spinning with a distaff and spindle. She holds the distaff in her left hand, drawing out the unspun wool with her right. Below hangs the spun yarn, at the end of which a spindle is suspended. The spindle is weighted by a 'whorl', which both enhances and stabilises the rotating action. The shank of the spindle is bound with ready-spun yarn, which is 'wound on' once the yarn grows to such a length that the spindle touches the ground. From a white-ground *oinochoe* (wine jug) made in Athens *c*.490 BC. Attributed to the Brygos Painter.

23 Skolt-Lappish women weaving on a warp-weighted loom.

3 Dress

24 Two bronze dress pins of the type used to fix the *peplos* at the shoulders. They measure about 18 inches long. Greek, from Boeotia, 8th century BC.

Soft furnishings were one commodity produced on the household loom; clothes were another. To a large extent the rectangular shape of the loom determined the shape of the clothes people wore. Today we are used to large factory-produced rolls of material, cut up into convenient shapes tailored to fit the body. The ancient loom, however, produced relatively short, rectangular pieces of cloth, which could be draped directly onto the body without the need for cutting to shape. Even the Roman toga, which was semicircular in shape, was woven in one piece. Thus there was no wastage and, in an age before the sewing machine, stitching was kept to a minimum. Pins, tucks and belts were used to keep the garment in place and, if necessary, to adjust the length.

Although at first sight, then, ancient drapery, for example on a statue, may seem complicated, in fact it is often very simple. Dress consisted basically of a loose-fitting tunic, short or long, which, if the weather or the occasion demanded, would be worn with an over-mantle. The latter usually took the form of a cloak, but in some cases a second tunic made of heavier material was worn over the first. Sculptors were particularly fond of exploiting the contrast between the folds of heavy and light materials when the two were worn together in this way.

Fashions changed very much more slowly in the ancient world than they do today. There was no rapid turnover of mass-produced, ready-to-wear clothes such as those which give rise to the here-today, gone-tomorrow styles of the modern fashion industry. The major distinctions in dress were between rich and poor, leisured and working classes. Nevertheless, there was scope for showing off. The dress of aristocratic Athenians in the latter half of the sixth century BC, for example, appears to have been particularly ostentatious, and for men even effeminate. This was

a period when Athens was under a strong oriental influence, encouraged by the tyrant Pisistratus who then ruled the city. Elaborately woven purple tunics were in vogue, worn with brilliant white tunics underneath. This sartorial extravagance, however, seems to have been brought to an end by the war with Persia, which introduced a new mood of conservatism into Athenian dress. In the opening years of the fifth century BC Athens was united with the rest of Greece in a bloody fight for freedom against the might of the Persian Empire, which was attempting to annexe the Greek mainland. The Greeks emerged the victors from this David-and-Goliath struggle. Athens, however, had been sacked; the sacred shrines of the city had been destroyed; many families had suffered loss of life and property. This was not the time for brash display of wealth, and there seems to have been a national reaction against the luxurious form of dress associated with the now hated Orient. In consequence, the dress of men in the fifth century BC became simpler and plainer than it had been in the previous century. Long tunics ceased to be worn, and in vase-painting and sculpture of the period men are shown wearing one garment only, a simple cloak (*himation*) which could be draped 25 in a variety of ways with varying degrees of modesty.

This form of dress was equated with the sober life-style of Sparta, and writing towards the end of the fifth century BC, the Athenian historian Thucydides remarks upon the contemporary dress of his countrymen: 'The Spartans were the first to adopt a moderate costume after the present fashion, and in other respects too the propertied class [i.e of Athens] changed their way of life to correspond as closely as possible with that of ordinary men.'

According to another Greek historian, Herodotus, a change of fashion in the dress of Athenian women came about in an even more

25 Greek dress: (a) the *peplos*; (b) the *chiton*; (c) the *himation*; (d) the *chlamys*.

sudden and sensational way. It is said to have occurred in the course of a dispute between Athens and the rival state of Aegina. The Athenians had dispatched an expedition against their enemy, with disastrous results. Only one man lived to carry home news of the calamity. When the women of Athens learnt of the loss of their husbands, brothers and sons, they crowded round the blameless messenger and, resentful of the fact that he alone should have survived, pulled out their dress-pins and stabbed him to death. This act of brutality outraged the city, and in order to punish the women and, presumably, to prevent them from using their dress-pins as weapons again, they were made to change from the Doric to the Ionic form of dress. Hitherto the Doric *peplos* had been worn, fastened on the shoulders by the long, menacing pins; henceforth women would wear the Ionic *chiton*, which could be fastened without them.

To judge from Athenian sculpture and vase-painting, the *chiton* was indeed becoming fashionable around the middle of the sixth century BC, when this particular conflict with Aegina probably took place. Whether the change in fashion happened in the manner Herodotus describes, however, seems very doubtful. The real reason is probably to be sought in the growing prosperity of Athens and in the influence of Pisistratus. For the *chiton*, which was in fact worn by both men and women at this time, was a form of dress imported from the east. Moreover, it was made from linen,

26 Diagrams of the toga and tunic worn by the 'Arringatore' (27). After Granger-Taylor.

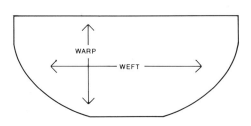
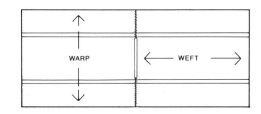

d

unlike the native *peplos* which was made from home-grown wool. Linen, being imported, was a costlier fabric and one which is likely to have appealed to the Athenians at a time when ostentation was not thought to be out of keeping with national pride.

The national dress of the Romans was the toga, worn over a tunic, and it was the right of all free-born citizens to wear it. Although stately, it was also very cumbersome, and only the leisured upper classes would have worn it for any length of time. Working people preferred a simple tunic, which is why the Roman historian Tacitus wrote of the 'tunic-clad populace'. Important Roman officials wore a toga with a purple stripe. The same distinctive marking was shown on the togas of boys up to the age of sixteen. At that age the youth assumed the plain *toga virilis*, dedicating his childhood garb to the household gods at a ceremony that marked an important stage in his upbringing.

An alternative form of cloak was the *pallium*, the Roman version of the Greek *himation*. During the Republic, however, this garment was frowned upon by those who thought Greek dress un-Roman and unmanly. The great general Scipio, who defeated the Carthaginians, is said to have been censured for sporting a *pallium* and sandals in the gymnasium in Sicily.

The *palla* was a garment worn by women

26, 27

27 The 'Arringatore' (orator). He wears a sleeveless tunic and over it a semicircular toga. Etruscan bronze, late 2nd century BC. Florence, Archaeological Museum.

28 Greek hairstyles.

and consisted of a deep rectangular shawl of woollen material draped around the shoulders and often drawn over the head. Together with the *stola*, a loose-fitting tunic akin to the Greek *chiton*, it constituted the traditional dress of Roman women.

Women in ancient Greece and Rome invariably wore their hair long, unless in Greece 28 they were of slave status or in mourning, in which case it was shorn into a bob. The long tresses of the free-born were rarely allowed to fall naturally, but were gathered into bunches or worn up according to the fashion of the day. Greek vases provide the best illustrations of female coiffure. Frequent use was made of a long, broad ribbon to bind the head and keep the hair in position. Alternatively the hair was enclosed in a net (*sakkos*). In Greece hair-nets 28c were made by a technique known today as 'sprang'. By this process parallel threads 29 stretched between two horizontal bars on a small hand-frame were plaited together to form a closely worked fabric.

The art of hairdressing in the ancient world achieved its most elaborate creations on the heads of the fashionable ladies of Imperial Rome. Some of the architectural constructions we find in the portrait sculpture of the day almost defy belief. The long-drawn-out sufferings of the woman who sat for hours at the hands of her hairdresser became part of the stock-in-trade of the Roman satirist. Many women probably preferred to effect the fanciful styles that fashion dictated by choosing the 30 easy option of a wig.

Men are by no means immune to vanity, and both Greece and Rome had their fair share of dandies. We have already remarked upon the luxury of male dress in the sixth century BC. This ostentation was reflected in the hair, which was worn long and fastened up with a gold brooch. Aristocratic men in particular were distinguished by their long hair at this time. Greek men grew beards and had no use

29 (*right*) A woman working 'sprang' on a hand-frame. 'Sprang' is made without a warp by twisting together threads stretched between two horizontal bars. From a 'six technique' *lekythos* (oil flask) made in Athens *c.* 480–470 BC.

30 (*far right*) Marble portrait bust of a woman with an elaborate hairstyle. Roman, *c.* AD 100–120.

31 Terracotta scent-bottles in the form of sandalled feet. Made in eastern Greece, 6th century BC.

for the razor, which was an article of female, rather than male toiletry. In Rome, by contrast, men appear to have shaved their beards until the emperor Hadrian inaugurated the fashion for them in the second century AD.

In keeping with the care taken with their hair, fashionable Roman ladies were also anxious to present the best possible countenance by the use of make-up. Again this feminine vanity was parodied by the poets, as a passage from Lucian illustrates:

If you could see women when they get up in the morning, you would think them less desirable than an ape. That is why they keep themselves closeted and will not show themselves to a man. Old hags and a chorus of serving-maids, no more glamorous than their mistress, surround her, plastering her wretched face with a variety of remedies. After all, a woman does not simply wash her sleep away with cold water and get on with the serious work of the day. Countless concoctions are used instead by way

32 A group of toilet articles. (From left) Roman silver spatulae, probably used for applying cosmetics; Roman scent-bottle of gold-banded glass, 1st century AD; Greek marble *pyxis* (cosmetic box), c.450–400 BC; Roman onyx scent-bottle; Roman ivory *pyxis* with carved decoration round the outside, 3rd century AD; and Roman ivory comb inscribed 'Modestina, farewell!'.

33 A lady seated in a wicker-work chair is attended by servants. From left to right, a servant dresses her mistress's hair; another holds a perfume jar; a third holds up a round mirror; a fourth stands by with a water jug. Roman marble relief from Neumagen, 3rd century AD. Trier, Rheinisches Landesmuseum.

31–33 of salves for improving her unpleasant complexion. Like participants in a public procession, each servant carries a different object: a silver bowl, a jug, a mirror, a variety of boxes, adequate for fitting out a chemist's shop, jars full of mischief, tooth-powders and stuff for darkening the eyelids.

Juvenal is another writer who cannot resist a jibe at the lengths to which women will go to improve their appearance. He sympathises with the husband who is tormented at night by the pungent cream with which his wife has smeared her face and the bread-pack that preserves the colour of her cheeks – precautions taken not to secure his own amorous interest but that of the lover whom she will seduce the next day.

Greek women, even the oppressively con-fined, also made use of make-up. Some husbands disapproved of it, however, and their advice was perhaps not altogether unkind when we consider that one of the commonest methods of lightening the complexion was the potentially dangerous use of powdered lead.

4 Children and Education

One of the striking aspects of Greek art and literature is the interest shown in depicting infants and young children. The following is a passage taken from the second play in Aeschylus's trilogy the *Oresteia*. Orestes, the son of the royal household at Mycenae, is feared dead, and his former nurse is given cause to reflect upon the past:

> I reared him, took him new-born from his
>   mother's arms.
> And oh! the times he shouted at me in the
>   night,
> Made me get up, and bothered me with this
>   and that –
> And all my hopes for nothing! Why, you
>   understand,
> A baby knows no better; you must nurse it,
>   then,
> Like a dumb animal, whatever way seems best.
> A child in the cradle can't explain what
>   troubles it;
> Whether it wants to eat, to drink, or to make
>   water,
> A baby's inside takes no orders; it's too young.
> Well, often I could tell; and often, too, I know,
> I guessed it wrong; and then I'd have to wash
>   his things,
> For nurse and laundress both were the same
>   pair of hands.
> So I did double duty; yes, and I brought up
> Orestes for his father. And now, to hear of this,
> Orestes dead!

These lines are a touching indication of the sentiment that could be aroused in the Greek mind by the subject of small children. We are given a visual reminder of this in the antics of childhood depicted on red-figured vases, and in particular in the scenes shown on a group of miniature wine jugs known as *choes*. These jugs were given to children on the occasion of a festival called the Anthesteria. It seems that they were given specifically to children of a certain age, perhaps as a token marking the child's passing out of infancy. One such jug shows an infant seated on a potty, who waves 37 his rattle at somebody to the left, perhaps as a signal that he has 'finished' and would like to be released to play with the go-cart propped up against the wall on the right. An actual example of such a potty was found by archae- 38 ologists excavating in the Athenian market-place in the 1950s.

The potty jug was painted with rapid brush-strokes and this spontaneity contributes considerably towards its success as an image. More laboured and much less certain is another scene depicting infancy, painted this time on the outside of a storage jar or *pelike*. It 39 shows a walking lesson in which a woman,

34 A nurse hands a baby to her mistress. The latter is seated on an armless chair (*klismos*), and at her feet stands a *kalathos* (wool basket). From a red-figured *hydria* (water jar) made in Athens *c.*440–430 BC.

35 A group of children's toys. (From left) terracotta whip-top, 8th century BC; terracotta dancing-doll holding castanets, made in Corinth *c.*350 BC; baby-feeder of black-glazed pottery with an inscription in Greek: 'drink, don't drop!', made in southern Italy, 4th century BC; miniature *chous* (wine jug) showing an infant crawling towards a table, made in Athens *c.*425–400 BC; terracotta rattle in the form of a pig, made in Cyprus, 3rd–2nd century BC.

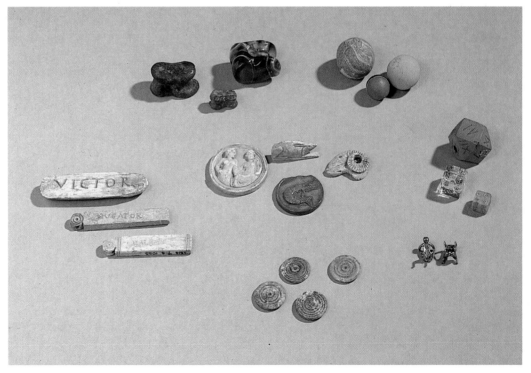

36 Gaming pieces. (Clockwise, from left) Roman ivory pieces inscribed *victor, nugator* (trifler) and *male(e)st* (bad luck); *astragali* (knucklebones) in bronze, glass and onyx – these were thrown like dice, each side having a different value; two Roman glass marbles from Egypt, and a Minoan pottery marble, 2000–1700 BC; Roman dice in faceted greenstone, rock-crystal and agate; Roman silver dice in the form of squatting figures, 1st–2nd century AD; Roman bone counters, 1st–2nd century AD, and (centre) Roman ivory counters in the form of two Muses, a hare, a ram and a lobster (probably 1st century AD).

37 Red-figured *chous* (miniature wine jug) showing a baby on a potty. The potty, mounted on a tall base, takes the form of a deep bowl in which the baby sits with his legs dangling out of two side holes. The child appears to be waving a rattle, perhaps as a signal that he has 'finished'. Against the 'wall' on the right there leans a push-cart, a favourite toy in ancient Greece. Made in Athens, *c.*440–430 BC.

38 (*opposite, above*) A modern child on an ancient potty, found during excavation of the Athenian *agora* (market place). Made in Athens *c.*580 BC. Athens, Agora Museum.

the child's nurse or mother, gives encouragement to the infant crawling at her feet. The male figure standing by is perhaps the child's grandfather who, having now retired from public life, is more inclined to take an interest in the upbringing of the future generation. The infant's father, by contrast, would have had very little to do with his offspring at this stage, delegating the task of rearing the child to his wife while he himself was concerned with matters outside the home. The aged figure in the vase-painting could alternatively be a *paidagogos*, that is to say a trusted slave who would eventually be responsible for supervising the education of the child.

The Romans were even more interested than the Greeks in the accurate representation of human types. They perfected the art of portraiture, and have handed down to us some of the most evocative images of childhood the world has ever seen.

These charming subjects should not, however, be allowed to obscure the harsher aspects of the ancient attitude to children. We read, for example, that the Spartans inspected their babies at birth for signs of mental or physical weakness. If an infirmity was discovered, the infant was tossed over a cliff to an untimely death. Sparta, admittedly, was an extreme

39 (*opposite, left*) A walking lesson, from a red-figured *pelike* (storage jar). Made in Athens *c.* 440–420 BC.

40 (*opposite, right*) Marble portrait-bust of a boy. Roman, 1st century AD.

case of a totalitarian society in which family life was rigidly subordinated to the needs of the state. The military-minded Spartans were certainly not alone, however, in practising infanticide, although the methods employed elsewhere were probably less violent. The most common was exposure, the unwanted baby being left to die in some remote spot. Alternatively, the infant could be abandoned in a public place where it might be found and reared, usually as a slave.

In myth, stories that focus upon the exposure of unwanted infants often have an unforeseen outcome. Most famous of all is the story of Oedipus, who grew up to murder his father and marry his mother, while in his tragedy *Ion* Euripides dramatises the story of a child exposed as an infant but found and brought up as a temple-boy, serving in the sanctuary of Apollo at Delphi. The play ends with a reconciliation between mother and son, but not before Ion narrowly escapes becoming an unwitting matricide. Rome itself was said to have been founded by the unwanted infant twins Romulus and Remus. According to the story, the babes were cast adrift on the River Tiber, but washed ashore at the foot of the Palatine Hill, one of the seven hills on which Rome was to be built. A she-wolf was the first to find them and they were raised by her.

In such stories as these, extraordinary circumstances usually accounted for the exposure of the infant. A prophecy that a child would grow up more powerful than the parent

41 The death of Priam. The aged king lies sprawled over the altar of Zeus where he had hoped to find refuge. Neoptolemos, in full armour, stands over the king and, ignoring his right to sanctuary, raises the body of Priam's grandson Astyanax like a club with which to batter the old man to death. Scene from a black-figured *amphora* made in Athens *c.* 540 BC.

was a popular motif, which perhaps expresses a genuine antagonism in the relationship between father and son. For fathers would ultimately become dependent upon their sons in old age. There was nothing like an old-age pension in the ancient world, and children were necessarily seen as a form of insurance. In literature, 'Who now is left to care for me in my old age?' is the often-repeated cry of bereaved and bewildered parents whose sons have died before them. There was no more tragic a father than Priam, king of Troy, who had reared fifty sons. The greatest of these, Hector, was destroyed in battle by the Greek hero Achilles. Priam himself died violently at the hands of Achilles's own son Neoptolemos.

Vase-painters chose to illustrate the death of Priam by combining it with the murder of Hector's son (Priam's grandson), Astyanax. Neoptolemos wields the body of Astyanax like a club with which to batter to death the old man, who has taken refuge at the altar of Zeus. The power of the image and its peculiar horror for the Greek mind lay in the simultaneous obliteration of generations: Priam the venerated patriarch is destroyed by the body of Astyanax, who had represented the hope for the future.

The relationship between grandfather and grandson was particularly close in the ancient world. Boys in ancient Greece were often named after their grandfather. The name was given at a ceremony known as the *amphidromia*, when the women of the house carried the child at a run around the hearth. Thus the memory of the old generation was kept alive in the new. In both Greece and Rome the naming ceremony marked the acceptance of the child into the family group. A period of seven to ten days was left between birth and the naming, during which the parents could judge whether the infant was likely to survive and perhaps decide whether or not to rear it. The physical acceptance of the child by the father was marked in Rome by the ceremony of *sublatus*, when the father raised the baby in his arms. This ritual act is shown on a sarcophagus relief representing various episodes in the upbringing of a Roman boy.

Schooling was a very much more haphazard affair in the ancient world than it usually is today. Only the sons of well-to-do families are likely to have received what was considered a full education. Schoolteachers were mostly employed on a fee-paying basis or were the slave property of the individual household. There were no hard-and-fast rules about when school life should begin, and the commonest age in both Greece and Rome was probably about seven.

The traditional education had been a training for war. The Homeric Achilles, who is in many ways the archetype of the properly educated young aristocrat, was taught music and athletics by his tutor, the centaur Chiron. Athletics strengthened the body and encouraged the competitive spirit that was needed in a successful warrior; while music, which extended to poetry and dance, was the embodiment of aristocratic cultural values. In fifth-century Athens every citizen was a potential soldier. At the age of eighteen or thereabouts the Athenian youth underwent a two-year period of intensive training for war. In Rome, in the late Republic and early Empire, military service remained a precondition of political office. Nowhere, however, was education more closely linked with the training of a warrior than at Sparta. Here boys were removed from family life at the age of seven to live in austere barracks, where they were subjected to a rigorous discipline. Even as infants, Spartans were systematically hardened by their upbringing. This is how the writer Plutarch describes the treatment they received at the hands of their no-nonsense nurses:

They reared infants without swaddling-bands, and thus left their limbs and figures free to develop; besides, they taught them to be contented and happy, not dainty about their food, nor fearful of the dark, nor afraid to be left alone, nor given to contemptible peevishness and whimpering. This is the

42

42 Scenes from the upbringing of a boy. On the left a mother suckles her infant while her husband looks on. The father is then shown holding his child, perhaps as a token of his acceptance of him into the family. Next the boy is shown at play, riding in a toy chariot drawn by a donkey. Finally the child is given his schooling. Marble relief from a Roman sarcophagus, 2nd century AD. Paris, Louvre.

reason why foreigners sometimes bought Spartan nurses for their children. Amycla, for instance, the nurse of the Athenian Alcibiades, is said to have been a Spartan.

Military training in Sparta culminated in the so-called *krypteia*, when the young Spartan was required to live apart from the community, hiding himself in the country. Hungry and alone, his existence was compared to that of a *lykanthropos* or werewolf. He lived by his wits, stealing food and preying at night on the Spartan slave-class (*helots*), one of whom at least he was expected to kill. This period of separation from normal life may be paralleled with similar rites practised by numerous other peoples, marking the boundary between boyhood and manhood.

Even Spartan girls were not exempt from the national obsession with physical fitness. The future mothers of Spartan warriors trained and competed against each other in athletic events. Such a practice would have been unthinkable in Athens, where girls were secluded like their mothers and apparently had no share in the education given to boys. Athenian girls were reared at home and 43 trained in the duties of the good housewife. If they received any more formal education, it would be given at home, most probably by an educated house-slave.

Boys too, like the heroic Achilles, might have a private tutor, but by the fifth century BC in Athens a number of professional teachers had set up schools specialising in different aspects of the curriculum. The *grammatistes* taught the basics of reading, writing and probably also arithmetic; the *kitharistes* taught 44 music; the *paidotribes* taught athletics. Not every Athenian father could afford to send his son to all three teachers, and many boys probably did not get beyond the lessons learnt at the *grammatistes*. These were, after all, likely to be of most practical use when it came to earning a living. Training in music and athletics,

however, was considered indispensable by the leisured class.

In the later stages of adolescence the sons of well-to-do families would receive a higher education in different forms of philosophy. At its most practical this consisted of lessons in rhetoric, where the would-be politician or contestant in a court of law was taught the art of presenting a plausible and articulate argument. There were some teachers, however, who concentrated on more abstract matters, such as geometry and moral philosophy. Such was Socrates, whose search for the truth and constant questioning of received opinion eventually led to his trial and execution for alleged impiety.

43 A group of terracottas from a girl's grave. These objects are perhaps toys which the dead girl has played with during her lifetime, or they may represent the deceased as a married woman, making up for the experience in real life that death had denied her. The models comprise a girl with moveable arms (one missing), a throne, a pair of miniature boots, a miniature *epinetron* (thigh-guard used in the preparation of wool) and a miniature *lebes gamikos* (marriage bowl), used in the wedding ceremony. Greek, made in Athens *c.*420 BC.

44 A music lesson. The bearded music-master sits holding a kind of lyre known as a *barbitos*. A pupil practising the double-pipes (*auloi*) sits facing him. To the left a seated youth plays the double-pipes to the apparent annoyance of a howling dog. Two boys amuse themselves with a pet cheetah. To the right a boy has just entered and waits his turn for a lesson in the double-pipes. Behind him stands a *paidagogos* (tutor) who has escorted his ward through the streets. Scene from a red-figured *hydria* (water jar) made in Athens c.480–470 BC.

'Captive Greece took her wild captor captive', quipped the Roman poet Horace. This is nowhere better demonstrated than in the development of Roman education, which by the first century BC had become fully Hellenised. Rome's conquest of the eastern Mediterranean had brought a large influx of Greeks into Italy. Many of these were educated beyond the common level, and their knowledge and teaching methods, particularly in literary studies, soon transformed Roman practice. Roman children were to grow up bilingual in Latin and Greek, and in higher education access to the Greek authors broadened immeasurably the hitherto rather restricted intellectual perspective of the Romans.

Like his Greek counterpart, however, the Roman scholar had first to learn the basics. The three 'Rs' were taught by the *litterator*, the Roman equivalent of the *grammatistes*. In this case, however, it seems that girls as well as boys were allowed to participate in the lessons. Such schools were known by the name *ludus*, the same word as is used for a game. This incongruity has puzzled ancient and modern commentators alike. One Roman etymologist, Festus, conjectured that the word was chosen to deceive children into thinking that school was more fun than it actually was. A modern suggestion, however, seems more likely, namely that the term derives from a time when games, in the sense of physical training for war, constituted the basis of Roman education. Physical exercise continued to be an important element in a Roman boy's education, which also included music and dancing, although these subjects were perhaps given less emphasis than they were by the more artistically minded Greeks.

5 Marriage and Death

In Greece it is likely that many brides met their husbands for the first time only on the wedding day. The betrothal was negotiated in the manner of a business transaction and only the respective fathers and their chosen witnesses need have been present. Thus, when on the evening of her wedding day the bride was taken from the familiar surroundings of her childhood home and removed to the house of her husband, far from being a joyous – or at least a bitter-sweet occasion – the wedding may have been a frightening, even traumatic experience.

Before the wedding, perhaps on the day before, the Greek bride sacrificed her childhood toys to Artemis. She was a virgin goddess, and it was thought appropriate that a girl should dedicate to her the objects associated with her own maidenhood. Probably on this day also, the water for the ritual bath taken by the bride (and, it seems, by the groom) was fetched in a tall vessel known as a *loutrophoros*. This distinctively shaped vessel with its tall neck, wide-flaring mouth and twin handles is often painted with a wedding scene. It may carry a funerary subject, however, for the *loutrophoros* was sometimes placed on the graves of those who died before marriage. The Greeks, like many peoples, appear to have felt that to die unmarried left the soul in an undesirable limbo. Wedlock was especially important for a woman in enabling her to fulfil her role in society as a wife and a mother. Men, too, were expected to father children and to provide a home for aged parents. A *loutrophoros*, therefore, acted as a token substitute for the married life that was denied by death.

On the wedding day itself there was sacrifice and feasting in the respective homes of the bride and groom. The bridal couple probably did not meet until the evening, when the bride was fetched by the groom, accompanied by his 'best man'. Vases often show the bride and groom, especially if they are a divine pair, riding in a chariot. In the mortal realm, however, this vehicle would have been used only at

45 Scene from a red-figured *pyxis* (cosmetic box) showing a marriage procession: the bride, accompanied by her groom, is driven to her new home in a chariot. Greek, 5th century BC. Attributed to the Marlay Painter.

46 A bride is taken to her new home in a country cart drawn by mules. The groom sits beside her and drives the cart. Behind the bridal pair sits the groom's 'best-man' (*parochos*). Black-figured *lekythos* (oil flask) made in Athens *c.*540 BC. Attributed to the Amasis Painter. New York, The Metropolitan Museum of Art.

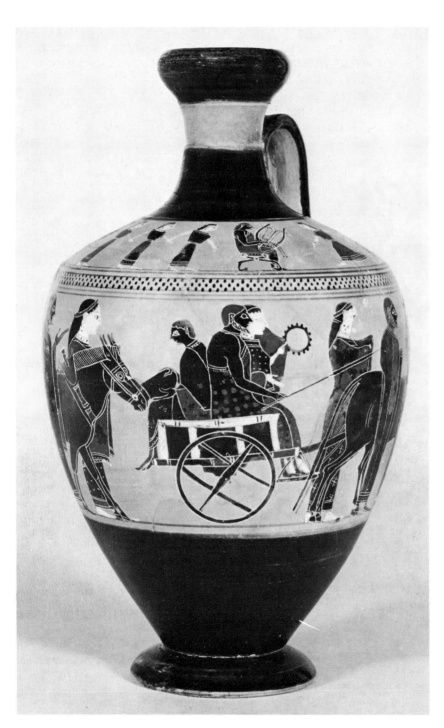

the most aristocratic of weddings. For the most part a simple country cart drawn by mules or 46 oxen was used for the wedding journey.

At the point when she crossed the threshold and was lifted onto the cart the bride's feelings may not, as has already been suggested, have been particularly joyful. We may perhaps invoke for the sake of comparison the sorrow expressed by the bride in modern Greek wedding dirges: 'Hide me, mother, hide me, so the stranger cannot take me', cries the bride in one lament. To which her helpless mother replies: 'How can I hide you, dear one, now you belong to him?'

The wedding cart made its way through the darkness to the groom's home. Here the newly-weds were met by the groom's mother, who came out bearing torches to light their way across the threshold. The groom led his pages 2–3 bride through the door towards the family hearth. At the place that represented the nucleus of the bride's future domestic life, the bride and groom knelt down and bowed their heads under a shower of nuts and sweetmeats (*katakysmata*), tokens of the prosperity it was hoped their union would bring to the house. All new residents of the household were first received through a ceremony at the hearth, and so placed under the protection of the household gods.

Following the ceremony of *katakysmata* the bride was conducted to the door of the bridal chamber amid a good deal of singing and ribaldry. The marriage was consummated and the next day the bride reappeared, now a member of a new household. On this day the two families came together – for the first time, it seems, during the wedding ceremonies – for a joint celebration in the groom's house. The bride's relatives brought presents with them and also, if it had not gone with the bride on the previous day, the dowry chest. The dowry was an amount of money or a collection of valuables that would be held in trust for the bride

47 Gold wedding ring showing *dextrarium iunctio* (joining of hands). Roman, 2nd–3rd century AD.

throughout her married life. Should her husband die prematurely or the marriage end in divorce, the dowry could be used to contract a second marriage for the bride.

It is unlikely that any subsequent marriage would involve the ceremonial ritual attending the first, for it was the bride's transition from virgin to wife that made marriage so momentous an event in her life. The Greek authors speak of the bride as a wild thing who must be tamed by marriage. Vase-painters frequently show the groom leading his bride by the wrist as though she were a captive. The idea of the bride as captive was nowhere more pronounced than at Sparta. This is how Plutarch describes the Spartan wedding ceremony:

For their marriages the women were carried off by force, not when they were small and unfit for wedlock, but when they were in full bloom and wholly ripe. After the woman was thus carried off, the bride's-maid, so called, took her in charge, cut her hair off close to the head, put a man's cloak and sandals on her, and laid her down on a pallet, on the floor, alone, in the dark. Then the bride-groom, not

48 The Roman marriage ceremony of *dextrarium iunctio.* Roman marble sarcophagus relief, 2nd century AD.

flown with wine or enfeebled by excesses, but composed and sober, after supping at his mess-table as usual, slipped stealthily into the room where the bride lay, loosed her virgin's zone, and bore her in his arms to the marriage-bed. Then, after spending a short time with his bride, he went away composedly to his usual quarters, there to sleep with the other young men.

This notion of ritual abduction is also present in the Roman ceremony, which in its broad outlines followed a pattern similar to that of the Athenian wedding. On the point of departing with her groom, the bride retreated into the arms of her mother and was forcibly removed. Once again the ritual underlined the bride's status as an initiate, as she passed from one stage of her life into another. The same may be said of the Roman bride's attire. The dress was an archaic form of tunic woven in a particular way. On her head she wore a veil of a distinctive orange colour, and her hair was dressed in an old-fashioned manner with six strands parted with the use of a bent iron spearhead. The boundary between virgin and wife was further marked by ceremonies at the threshold of her husband's home. When the wedding procession arrived, the bride smeared the doorposts with oil and fat and wreathed them with wool. Then, like the modern bride, she was carried across the threshold.

To die unburied and unmourned in the ancient world was a misfortune greater than death itself. Funerary rites might be elaborate and costly in the case of the rich, or simple and modest in the case of the poor. The intention, however, was always the same, to ensure the passage of the soul into the after-life. According to mythology the soul was led by the messenger-god Hermes (Roman Mercury) to the River Styx, marking the great divide between the living and the dead. There Charon the boatman waited to ferry the souls across into Hades or, if they were particularly fortunate, the Islands of the Blessed.

49 Three white-ground *lekythoi* (oil flasks) showing funerary subjects: (left) the deceased, laid out on a bier, is mourned by his family; (centre) Charon the ferryman reaches out for the hand of a departing soul whom he will transport across the Styx, the great river separating the living from the dead; (right) a woman performs a commemorative rite at a tomb, decking the stele marking the grave with ribbons. The youth is perhaps intended to represent the deceased. All made in Athens in the first half of the 5th century BC. The vase on the left is attributed to the Sabouroff Painter; the others to the Reed Painter.

It would be simplistic to assume that everyone held so naïve a notion of life after death. Neither the Greeks nor the Romans had any very clear or uniform idea of life in the hereafter, other than that the dead were a community of souls dependent for their continued well-being on the solicitations of the living. In both Greece and Rome the dead were kept alive, as it were, on appointed days after the funeral and throughout the year with offerings of food and libations. It is quite a common feature of Greek and Roman burials to find a pipe inserted into the tomb, through which food and drink were poured into the chamber below. By this sharing of meals the memory of the dead was incorporated into the everyday lives of the family to which they belonged.

In poetry and epitaph the untimely death of a boy or girl before marriage was often expressed symbolically as a marriage into the Underworld. In more general terms also, the funeral ceremony with its washing and dressing of the body, garlands and torches, dirges and journey by cart to a new 'home', may be seen to follow a pattern similar to the wedding. The ancients were themselves fully aware of this parallel, and saw marriage and death, wedding and funeral as similar experiences. The departing soul, like the bride, was treated as an initiate passing from one phase of being into the next.

Funerary rites (and, for that matter, marriage rites too) were not only necessary for the 'initiate', they were also a means of channelling the grief and sense of loss that afflicted those who were left behind. Moreover, those who were closely associated with the deceased were themselves considered to be polluted by death. Physical contact with the corpse, in particular, was thought to contaminate the living with its stigma. Thus, as death separated the deceased from life and the living, so contact with the deceased, and the accompanying feelings that death aroused in the heart and mind of the bereaved, set the latter apart from the rest of the community. The wearing of black, the ritual cutting of hair, the tearing and defilement of the flesh and loud lamentation all served to release the passion of the mourners and, at the same time, to mark their separation from the rest of society. Through the conventional pattern of funerary ritual the mourner underwent his or her own 'rite of passage', experiencing a period of separation, transition and eventual reincorporation into the living community.

The burial rites were carried out by the deceased's own kin. The task of laying out the body was normally given to the women of the house. The corpse was washed and anointed and then wrapped in a shroud. In the case of a Roman citizen the body was usually dressed in a toga. In Rome, and in the later period in Greece, a coin was placed in the mouth. This was to pay the fare demanded by Charon. A crown or wreath was placed upon the head.

Once it had been dressed, the corpse was placed on a couch. The 'lying in state' that followed was called *prothesis* in Greece. The Romans used the verb *collocare* to describe the same event. The purpose was to allow for the funeral lamentation during which relatives would gather in the house to pour out their

50 Red-figured *loutrophoros* showing women mourning around a bier. The women wear black and their hair is cut short. The *loutrophoros* was used to fetch water for the ceremonial marriage-bath taken by brides and grooms, but it was also placed on the tombs of those who died unmarried, and it may therefore depict scenes of either marriage or death. Made in Athens c.430 BC.

52 (*right*) The deceased, reclining as if he were an impassive observer of his own funeral, is carried on a bier. The procession is led by musicians, while the dead man's family follows behind. Roman sarcophagus relief, possibly 1st century BC or 1st century AD. Rome, Museo Aquilano.

grief in mourning. *Prothesis* usually lasted one day in Greece but up to seven in Rome, after which the body was carried to the tomb. The corpse was placed on a bier carried by pall-bearers or on a cart. The degree of luxury displayed by the funerary cortège varied according to the wealth and status of the deceased. Throughout Classical antiquity laws were passed in an attempt to curb what the authorities considered to be undesirable excess in funeral expenditure. Funerals in Athens, for example, provided the normally confined women of the town with the chance to show off their finery. The proceedings of one law-court case record how an illicit love affair started when the wife of a certain Eratosthenes

51

caught the roving eye of an admirer at a funeral.

Funerals also gave mourners the opportunity to make a public demonstration of family solidarity, and it seems individual families would attempt to out-do each other in the display of wealth. Periodically the showy habit of hiring professional mourners had to be banned, because of the rumpus they created.

In the case of certain distinguished individuals, sumptuary laws were relaxed in order to provide the deceased with a public funeral. In Rome during the Imperial period such a state occasion was normally reserved for the emperor. Under the Republic, however, the dead of noble Roman families were often placed in the Forum. Patrician families were also in the habit of keeping masks resembling their ancestors in the house. At funerals these are said to have been worn by members of the cortège. This practice continued into the Empire, and at the emperor Vespasian's funeral a figure is said to have walked in the procession wearing a mask in the likeness of the dead ruler, impersonating him with words and gestures.

52

51 The deceased is conveyed to the tomb on a cart drawn by mules. A woman, perhaps the dead man's wife, is shown seated on the vehicle. Scene from a black-figured *kantharos* (drinking cup) made in Athens *c.* 520 BC. Paris, Bibliothèque Nationale.

6 Greek Athletic and Dramatic Festivals

The Greek and Roman year was crammed with public festivals, which, like weddings and funerals, followed a traditional pattern of events, made sacred through repeated usage. The essence of ancient religion is to be found in ritual rather than dogma, and this was a necessary part of all religious activity, whether a simple votive offering made at a shrine or the elaborate ceremonial of state festival.

53 Sacrifice, more than any other religious activity, was carried out with meticulous observance of closely defined rules; indeed, the efficacy of the ritual was thought to depend upon the right words and the right actions being spoken and performed at the right moment of the proceedings. The purpose of sacrifice was to communicate with the gods, and there was no more effective means of doing this than through blood-sacrifice.

The Parthenon frieze affords us a unique illustration of a community – in this instance the community of Athens – soliciting the attention of its gods through the medium of sacrifice. The frieze represents the procession that was the culmination of the Great Panathenaic 54 Festival, held every four years (there was a lesser festival held every year) to celebrate the birthday of Athena, patron-goddess of the city. The gods are shown seated and facing the procession, which is led by young women carrying jugs and bowls for the pouring of ritual libations of wine. Behind them come men leading sheep and cattle as sacrificial victims. These, together with the wine and barley meal sprinkled upon the altar, constitute the sacrificial meal which the gods will share with their mortal hosts, so effecting a union between the normally separate worlds of mortal and divine.

The procession and the sacrifice that fol-

lowed were two ways of attracting the attention of the gods and communicating with them; another was competition – athletic, musical or dramatic – dedicated to a presiding deity and performed, as it were, in the presence of the god or goddess.

Athletics

The games had an important role to play in the religion of ancient Greece. The oldest athletic festival was that held at Olympia, where there had been a sanctuary dedicated to Zeus from early times. By the middle of the sixth century BC there were in addition three other major athletic festivals, each based at the sanctuary

53 A boar bound with a broad ribbon is led to sacrifice. Roman bronze relief, 1st or 2nd century AD.

54 The Panathenaic Way, leading to the Acropolis through the *agora* (marketplace) of Athens, formed part of the route of the procession of the Great Panathenaic Festival.

of the particular god in whose honour the games were celebrated. The Pythian Games held in honour of Apollo took place at Delphi every four years; the sacred grove of Nemea sheltered the sanctuary of Nemean Zeus and was visited by athletes at a festival held every two years, and the Isthmian Games were also held every two years, at the sanctuary of Poseidon on the Isthmus of Corinth. These festivals were arranged so that at least one of the Panhellenic Games fell every year, and together they were known as the *periodos*, or circuit.

The ancient Greeks were by nature competitive. In public life a man valued his reputation above all things, and by excelling over his social peers the successful athlete gained honour (*timē*). Personal honour was closely bound up with that of family and state, so that at one of the great Panhellenic Games a competitor risked not only his own reputation but also that of his kinsmen and fellow citizens. Rivalry between the small independent city-states of ancient Greece was no less intense than it is among participating nations at the modern Olympic Games. The ancient Olympic festival was set against a background of frequent political discord. Every fourth spring, before the games, heralds were sent round calling upon the Greeks to attend under the protection of a sacred truce. The truce never actually prevented a war, but it did guarantee an unhindered passage for people travelling to Olympia. This meant that even in times of extreme political crisis the games could go on; and so they did, uninterrupted for nearly a thousand years.

A victor at the games was rewarded with a wreath. At Olympia this was made from olive twigs cut from a sacred tree growing in the sanctuary. Civic pride, however, often ensured that on return to their city successful athletes would also receive a material award. Already by the end of the fifth century BC there had

grown up a class of professional athletes who went from city to city in search of the rich rewards that a victory at the games might bring. This development was eventually to undermine the ideal of noble amateurism on which Greek athletic competition was founded. In the Hellenistic and Roman periods professional athletes drawn from all levels of society dominated the games with their specialist training and techniques.

In addition to the Panhellenic Games there were numerous festivals featuring athletic events. Of these the Great Panathenaia was the most important. Although it never acquired Panhellenic status, it was of more than just local interest, with events for both citizens and outsiders. The happy victor took home a large quantity of olive oil in a jar known today as a Panathenaic amphora.

The Panathenaic Games featured events for all ages: boys, 'beardless youths' and men. The traditional education of boys from well-to-do families in Greece placed great emphasis on athletics. In early times instruction would have been given by the boy's father or a private tutor. By the fifth century BC, however, it had become common practice for Athenians to send their sons to a special school called a *palaistra*, or wrestling school. Here boys and youths were given expert tuition by a professional instructor (*paidotribes*), who charged a fee for his services. Much care was taken by parents over the selection of a *palaistra*, and it seems there were a number to choose from.

55 Panathenaic prize-*amphora* showing a horse-race. Such vessels were made especially to hold the olive oil awarded to victors in the Panathenaic Games. Made in Athens *c.* 500–490 BC. Attributed to the Eucharides Painter.

56 Athletes, two with javelins, one with a discus, and one with jumping weights used in the long jump to increase the distance. Scene from a Panathenaic *amphora* made in Athens *c.* 530–520 BC. Attributed to the Euphiletos Painter.

57 Athlete's bronze toilet set consisting of an *aryballos* (oil flask) and two strigils, used for scraping the body clean after exercise. Roman, 1st or 2nd century AD.

The *palaistra* was probably modelled along the same lines as the Greek house, with an enlarged courtyard serving as a sports ground, enclosed by a wall or by rooms built along one or more sides. These rooms looked onto the practice ground, with perhaps the addition of a verandah offering shade from the sun or shelter in bad weather. The rooms around the court provided a dressing room, washing facilities and a place where equipment could be stored when not in use. Here we might also expect to find a lodging for the *paidotribes*.

Besides the *palaistra* there was the *gymnasion*, which was not a private institution but one open to the public. Today we think of a gymnasium as a single building, roofed over and equipped for the sole purpose of physical exercise. In antiquity the word had rather a different meaning, literally, 'an exercise for which you strip', and it came by association to be used to refer to the place where the exercise took place.

The earliest gymnasia were probably just open areas of ground adjoining a sacred grove. At the end of the sixth century BC Athens had three gymnasia: the Academy, the Lyceum and another in the region known as Kynosarges. All three had been founded outside the city, where open terrain provided space for practising running and throwing the discus and javelin, events which were impractical for the restricted *palaistra* within the city walls. Moreover, the physical education of young Athenians culminated in a period of intensive military drill. The open spaces of the Academy and Lyceum were therefore used to train the Athenian cavalry and infantry.

Thirsty athletes needed water to drink and for bathing after exercise, and this was also taken into account when a site for a gymnasium was chosen. The Academy at Athens was situated on the road leading from the Dipylon Gate to the River Kephissos. The Lyceum was to be found on the east side of the city, close to the spring of the Eridanos, while the gymnasium at Kynosarges was located further to the south-east, on the south bank of the River Ilissos, near the celebrated spring of Kallirrhoe. The proximity of water also had the advantage of encouraging the growth of trees to provide shade against the sun, as well as other vegetation. The Academy was celebrated throughout antiquity for its beauty. The fifth-century dramatist Aristophanes describes in his play *The Clouds* how the young athlete may find relaxation under the sacred olive trees, enjoying the scent of the white poplar and 'carefree bindweed'. It was probably these natural advantages that attracted Plato when he founded his school of philosophy at the Academy in 387 BC. Later, in the first century BC, Cicero described it simply as 'the noblest gymnasium in the world'.

Music

In ancient Greece music and poetry were closely linked. Poetry was not meant for private reading but for public performance: the words were sung or chanted, often with an instrumental accompaniment and sometimes with dancing as well. Thus the Greek word *mousikē* had a much wider range of meaning than our 'music'. Indeed, in its broadest sense,

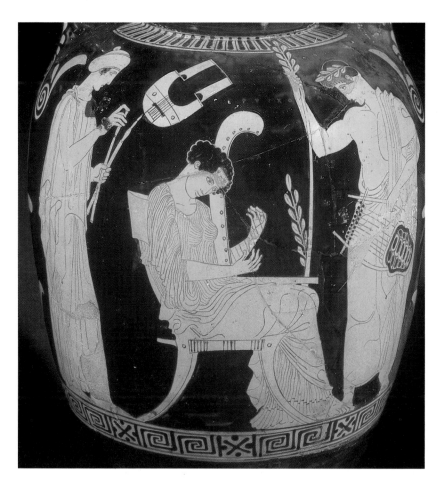

58 A woman playing a harp-like instrument. On the left a second woman holds a pair of *auloi* (double-pipes); on the right a youth holds a lyre. In the background there hangs a lyre-type instrument known as a cradle-*kithara*. Scene from a red-figured *amphora* made in Athens *c*.440 BC. Attributed to the Peleus Painter.

mousikē defies definition, since the term could be applied to any of the arts governed by Apollo and the Muses. Their sphere of patronage included nearly every human artistic and intellectual activity, from singing and dancing to philosophical discourse. The theatre, strictly speaking, was not among the arts over which the Muses presided, since it had its own patron in the god Dionysus. We cannot, however, make any rigid distinction between music and drama, since song and dance were a vital and inseparable part of dramatic performance.

In daily life music had an all-pervasive importance. At most social events there was likely to be some kind of musical performance, even if a musical event was not itself the reason for the gathering. There were joyful songs to celebrate childbirth; sad lamentations after death; work-songs for harvesting, grinding grain and weaving; drinking songs; love songs; songs for worship; even songs for curing illness.

Religious festivals often featured musical contests. Besides the performance of older works such as the Homeric epics, the annual round of festivals also gave a number of new compositions their first hearing. Successful entries were likely to be remembered, and repeated performance at *symposia* ensured them a place in the popular tradition. No work was guaranteed more than a single performance, however, and many must have passed into oblivion soon after they were composed.

Although we can be certain of the importance of music in Greek life, our knowledge of what the music was actually like is sadly deficient. Consider for example Fig. 59, which shows a musician wearing the ceremonial dress customary for someone competing at a festival. His head tilts back and his lips are parted to indicate that he is singing. He stops the strings of an instrument known as a *kithara* with the fingers of his left hand, while in the right he holds a plectrum. For all the detail in this vase-painting, there is no inscription to indicate what song was being sung or the tune that was played. Such scenes serve only as a silent reminder of music that is lost and will probably never be recovered. It has long been known that the ancient Greeks possessed a system of musical notation, evidence of which is preserved in the works of the ancient musical theorists, in fragments of papyrus and in stone inscriptions. It was once hoped that archaeologists would eventually uncover enough musically annotated texts for it to be possible to reconstruct the musical settings

59 A youth plays the *kithara*, striking the strings with a plectrum and lifting back his head and opening his mouth wide in song. From a red-figured *amphora* made in Athens *c*.490 BC. Attributed to the Berlin Painter. New York, The Metropolitan Museum of Art.

60 A youth playing the *auloi* (double-pipes). The musician stands on a podium and wears a long flowing tunic with a short jerkin decorated with a bold diaper pattern. A leather strap (*phorbeia*) runs around his face. This was perhaps a means of preventing the cheeks from puffing out while blowing into the reed mouthpiece of the instrument. From a red-figured *amphora* made in Athens *c*.480 BC. Attributed to the Kleophrades Painter.

61 (*opposite, left*) Reconstructions of the lyre and the *kithara* (back view). The distinctive feature of the lyre was a sound-box made from the shell of a tortoise with a resonant hide stretched over the hollow underside. Strings of gut or sinew were extended over the sound-box and held in tension by a cross-bar. Leather thongs or pegs served as a tuning device. The normal number of strings was seven. The *kithara* was a more elaborate, deeper-sounding version of the lyre. The larger, normally flat-bottomed sound-box was made out of wood and was extended upwards forming two arms which supported the cross-bar.

used by the great poets and dramatists. What has been discovered to date, however, is extremely fragmentary and belongs for the most part to the Hellenistic or Roman periods. Only one scrap of notation provides a possible setting for a piece of fifth-century drama: lines 338–344 of Euripides's *Orestes* are given with musical notation on a fragment of papyrus dated to around 200 BC. Unfortunately, it is impossible to tell whether the text preserves a part of the original fifth-century production or a later arrangement.

In any case, musical notation probably had more to do with musical theory than practice.

Our earliest literary reference to it is in the theoretical treatise of Aristoxenus (*fl.* 320 BC). Theory and practice were not integrated as they are today, for by the fifth century BC Greek musical theory had been developed into an independent science, forming a branch of Pythagorean mathematics and astronomy. The business of teaching music and playing went on without the use of a written score, at least to judge from vase-paintings.

Instrumental music in Classical Athens seems to have been unwritten. The accompaniment to any given piece must have been largely improvised for each performance, and

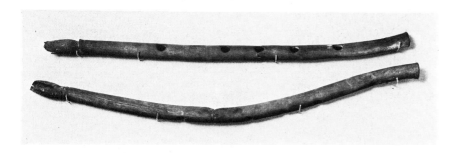

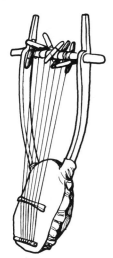

62 Two *auloi* made of sycamore wood. The *aulos* was the principal wind instrument of ancient Greece. Often mistakenly called a flute, it was in fact fitted with a reed mouthpiece and was therefore more akin to the modern oboe. The instrument was usually played in pairs. Probably 5th or 4th century BC.

63 A bearded rhapsode recites from a podium. From his mouth issue the first words of a poem: 'Once upon a time in Tiryns...'. From a red-figured *amphora* made in Athens c.480 BC. Attributed to the Kleophrades Painter.

we have no way of recalling it. If we ask, 'what did the music of Periclean Athens sound like?', the answer is that we simply do not know. Even to ask what kind of music it was, is to pose an almost unanswerable question. One thing modern scholars are agreed upon, however, is that in the whole period of ancient Greek music there was never anything comparable with the complex harmony of modern choral and orchestral arrangements. When voices sang together they sang in unison, and for the most part it was customary for voice and musical instrument to follow the same melodic line. This had the advantage of making the words sound as clear as possible. Although instrumental music was enjoyed for its own sake and festivals featured competitions for solo instrumentalists, the primary function of music was to provide a setting for the words of a song. It was clearly a priority that the music should enhance the words and their meaning by playing along with the voice, rather than obscure the vocal line, for example by creating an independent melody in counterpoint.

The Theatre

Drama in ancient Greece formed part of the celebration of some religious festivals, and the City Dionysia held every spring in honour of Dionysus Eleutherius was the principal such festival in Athens. It took the form of a competition, with prizes for the winners. In the tragedy contest, for example, three poets entered four plays each – three tragedies and a satyr-play, a form of farce involving actors dressed in satyr costume.

The physical setting for the City Dionysia in the fifth century BC was the Theatre of Dionysus on the south-east side of the Acropolis. An 64 auditorium was terraced out of the steep slope of the hill. Seats were arranged in narrow tiers rising one above the other, overlooking a circular dance-floor or 'orchestra'. In performance this was the space commanded by the chorus, since in Greek drama there were not only actors (usually three) but also a dozen or more 'song and dance men'.

If we were to strip everything away from the Greek theatre except the orchestra, we should still retain the essential element. The dance-floor was probably as old as Greek civilisation itself, in its simplest form being no more than the circular threshing floor still used for dancing in rural parts of Greece today. The regular pattern of circular dances became an irresistible motif for vase-painters, who often exploited it to decorate the rounded surface of a pot.

By the fifth century BC the choral dances of Greek tragedy were not circular, it seems, but moved in straight lines. Nevertheless, tradition demanded that the circular shape of the orchestra be retained. In any case it was not only tragedy that was performed in the fifth-century Theatre of Dionysus, but also a form of choral song and dance known as 'dithyramb', in which each of the ten tribes of Athens entered a chorus of fifty men and one of fifty boys, who danced in a circle miming their song in the movements of their hands.

As we see it today, the Theatre of Dionysus no longer provides a good illustration of the Classical Greek theatre. A better impression is to be had from the Hellenistic theatre at Epidaurus, where the circular form of the orchestra has been preserved and where modern productions of the Classical plays are still staged. At Athens, the orchestra has been cut across by the intrusion of a Roman stage building, which marks not only an important alteration in the physical appearance of the theatre but also a radical change in the idea of dramatic performance. The introduction of a stage building had already occurred in the Hellenistic period and had the effect of raising the actors above ground level, separating them from the chorus and audience below.

66 (above) A modern production of Aristophanes's *Lysistrata* at Epidaurus.

64 (left, above) The Theatre of Dionysus on the south-east slope of the Acropolis.

65 (left) A comic dance in padded costume was popular in Greece during the 7th and 6th centuries BC, and is thought to have been a forerunner of later forms of comedy. Here padded male dancers are joined by naked females. From a black-figured *amphora* made in Corinth around 550 BC.

This division was totally alien to the idea of theatre to which the fifth-century Athenian was accustomed, where chorus and actor freely interacted on the same horizontal plane.

Another feature of the Classical Greek theatre was a construction called a *skēnē* on the far side of the orchestra from the audience. This was almost certainly made out of wood, and so none has survived. It would have had a central doorway with large double doors opening inwards, and probably also two smaller doorways on either side of the main one. The roof must have been flat so as to allow for the occasional appearance of an actor on, or from, the top of a building. For example, the opening lines of the *Agamemnon*, the first play of the *Oresteia*, are delivered by the watchman from the roof of Agamemnon's palace. The architectural façade of the *skēnē* served to represent whatever was required for the action of the play: a palace, perhaps, or a temple.

In addition to the *skēnē* there was possibly also a low wooden platform immediately in front of the main doorway; not, it must be emphasised, a stage, but a step or two which actors could use for dramatic effect. One of its functions was to accommodate the mechanical device known as an *ekkyklēma*, a sort of low trolley which could be rolled or wheeled out through the central doorway. The purpose of this was to bring into the audience's view a tableau of the outcome of events that had taken place out of sight inside the building. Such, for example, was Clytemnestra's murder of her husband Agamemnon and his concubine Cassandra in the *Oresteia*. The line: 'I stand where I struck, over the work that I have done', would have been delivered over the bodies of Agamemnon and Cassandra sprawled at the feet of the avenging queen. As they issued through the doorway and rolled into the audience's view, the effect must have been as weird as it was impressive.

Another mechanical device, which was apparently exploited to hilarious effect in comedy but which would also have had a part to play in tragedy, was the *mechanē*, a form of crane used to suspend actors in mid-air. In Aristophanes's *Clouds*, an outrageous parody of the philosopher Socrates begins when a would-be pupil called Strepsiades first encounters his teacher deep in abstract thought, suspended above the ground in a basket.

Comedy, like tragedy, was staged at religious festivals, including the City Dionysia and, from around 450 BC, the festival of the Lenaia held in January. Here too the chorus had a prominent role, often in the plays of Aristophanes being composed of men in animal costume – frogs, for example, or birds. Aristophanes's surviving plays reveal a sophisticated and often bitingly satirical humour combined with a good deal of unashamed obscenity. The costume of the comic actor consisted of a pair of loose-fitting

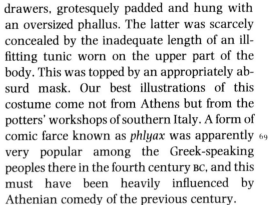

drawers, grotesquely padded and hung with an oversized phallus. The latter was scarcely concealed by the inadequate length of an ill-fitting tunic worn on the upper part of the body. This was topped by an appropriately absurd mask. Our best illustrations of this costume come not from Athens but from the potters' workshops of southern Italy. A form of comic farce known as *phlyax* was apparently 69 very popular among the Greek-speaking peoples there in the fourth century BC, and this must have been heavily influenced by Athenian comedy of the previous century.

By the fourth century BC the great age of Athenian drama was over. None of the authors of the later forms of so-called Middle and New comedy was ever the equal of Aristophanes, and although the old tragedies were revered as classics and were given repeated performances, no new playwright came forward to rival the stature of the great fifth-century tragedians.

67 (*above left*) A chorus of men in bird costume dance to the music of a pipe-player. Animal choruses became a common feature of later Athenian comedy as, for example, in *The Birds* by Aristophanes, first produced in 414 BC. Black-figured *chous* (wine jug) made in Athens *c.*510–490 BC. Attributed to the Gela Painter.

68 (*above right*) A comic actor playing the part of a runaway slave. The miscreant slave is first met with in the comedies of Aristophanes and goes on to become one of the stock characters of ancient comedy. Here he is shown on an altar where he has taken refuge from an irate master. Terracotta made in Athens *c.*350–325 BC.

69 (*left*) Actors in comic costume in a performance apparently parodying the story of the healing of the centaur Chiron. The wounded centaur, whose name is inscribed above, is pushed and pulled on to a stage building, which probably represents a healing sanctuary. This form of farce, known as *phlyax*, was popular in southern Italy in the 4th century BC. From a red-figured *bell-krater* (bowl for mixing wine and water) made in Apulia, southern Italy, *c.*380 BC.

7 Roman Games and Gladiators

Like the Greek theatre, the Roman Games (*ludi*) had a religious context. The oldest and grandest were the Ludi Magni, which in early times were vowed in honour of Jupiter Optimus Maximus by successful generals celebrating a victory. Gradually, it seems, these games became an annual event, and by 366 BC they were being held every September. Later still, more games were instituted on an annual basis and they became a permanent and frequent element in the Roman religious calendar. By the late Republic the games were organised and paid for by serving magistrates who sought to further their own careers by pleasing the electorate through the entertainment they provided. Inevitably, therefore, the original idea of the games as a celebration in honour of the gods was eclipsed by their increasing role as an advertisement promoting the ambitions of men. *Panem et circenses* (bread and circuses), as Juvenal put it, were what the people came to expect as of right, and men in public office had to dig deep into their own pockets to oblige them.

The games consisted traditionally of a grand procession followed by chariot racing, staged animal hunts and drama. Gladiatorial combat was not at first a part of the games, having, as we shall see, a different origin. Theatrical productions ranged from Roman adaptations of Greek forms of drama to more popular types of farce. By the second century BC, there were on the one hand the Greek-style comedies of Terence and Plautus and on the other the so-called mimes, a particularly popular and peculiarly Roman blend of satire and buffoonery, performed without the usual mask. The Roman authorities were fully aware not only of the political expediency of these entertainments, but also of their potential as 'opium of the people'. The emperor Augustus is reported to have censured a popular actor in the mimes called Pylades, whose petty quarrels and jealousies had become the talk of Rome. With calculated coolness he replied: 'It is to your advantage, Caesar, that the people should keep their thoughts on us.'

Chariot racing in Rome was staged in the Circus Maximus, situated in a valley between the Palatine and Aventine hills. Races had been held here since the days when Rome was ruled by kings. In time the race track was enlarged and equipped with seats for the spectators. The crowd, it seems, was composed of both men and women, sitting together: at the theatre and the amphitheatre the sexes were separated. The Circus underwent successive modifications and improvements. In 46 BC, for example, Julius Caesar enlarged it to the east and west and surrounded it with a moat filled with water, presumably to make the area safe for spectators watching wild beast shows. It was not, after all, only chariot races that took place in the Circus. Earlier, in 55 BC, iron barriers separating the crowd from the sports

70 Three actors from a Roman 'mime'. By about 50 BC a form of farce known as *mimus* had gained great popularity, particularly among the lower classes living in the towns. The Roman 'mime' differed from Greek comedy in that actors did not wear masks, and female parts were played by women rather than by men in female costume. Roman terracottas, 1st century AD.

ground had given way at the games sponsored by Pompey in which armed Spanish Gaetulians were set to fight twenty elephants. Under the Empire such bloody spectacles were usually reserved for the amphitheatre.

The chariot races themselves became highly organised affairs. Independently owned stables were established to cater for the demand for trained racehorses, and these were hired out, together with their drivers, to the magistrates funding the games. Passionate rivalry grew up between the stables. They de-

veloped their own followings, which were known as 'factions', identified by their colours: the Reds, Whites, Blues and Greens.

The Romans followed the Greek practice of beginning their races with a staggered start so as to make allowance for the greater distance run on the outside of the track. A central barrier (*spina*) separated the two sides of the race track. The most dramatic moments of the race usually came on the turn, where if a team were driven too wide of the post it was in danger of being overtaken on the inside, but if the

71 A reconstructed model of the Circus Maximus, Rome. Rome, Museo della Civiltà Romana.

72

title page

driver cut it too fine, then he ran the risk of crashing. There were different events for chariots drawn by two, three or four horses, and events for both team and individual entries. The charioteers themselves were mostly slaves, many of whom must have been born to the stables from fathers who had followed the same profession. Successful charioteers, like gladiators, became the darlings of the people and might make enough profit to buy their freedom.

It was no doubt the adulation of the crowd that prompted the eccentric emperor Nero to practise the sport. The 211th Olympic Games were postponed from AD 65 to AD 67 so that he could compete in the chariot race. Although he fell from the chariot and the race had to be stopped while he remounted, and in spite of the fact that even then he failed to finish, nevertheless he was declared the winner on the grounds that if he had finished, then he would have won.

The Amphitheatre

The bloodier spectacles, or *munera*, as they were known, were also religious in origin. They were first held at funerals as a blood-offering to the deceased. Gladiators were sometimes known as *bustuarii*, or 'funeral men', and throughout their history the Romans continued to honour the memory of great men with gladiatorial contests. In the course of time, however, like the *ludi*, the *munera* became secularised as men in public life sought to secure the favour of the mob by pandering to its morbid tastes. Under the Empire it was the emperor's privilege to exploit

72 Terracotta lamp showing a chariot race in the Circus Maximus, Rome. Round the outside are shown (top left) the spectators; (top right) the *carcares* or starting gates, and (bottom) the elaborate barrier, called a *spina*, round which the chariots raced. Roman, made in Italy in the late 2nd or early 3rd century BC.

the propaganda potential of *munera* by giving the most frequent, as well as the grandest, shows while at the same time limiting the number and size of those that could be given by others.

Rome did not acquire a stone-built arena until fairly late. At first *munera* were held in the Circus or in the Forum. The first permanent amphitheatre was built in 29 BC but was destroyed in the great fire of AD 64. It was replaced by the Colosseum, begun under Vespasian but not dedicated until AD 80 in the reign of the emperor Titus. Today the building, with its imposing arches arranged in three tiers, stands as one of the most remarkable products of Roman engineering. It is calculated to have had seating capacity for 45,000 people and standing room for a further 5,000. Underground there were cages for the wild beasts and a water system capable of flooding the arena for mock sea-battles.

The organisation of *munera* left nothing to chance. In the Italian townships and the provinces of the Empire the local magistrates who funded the shows as part of their civic duty contracted the job of mounting the events to a middleman, or *lanista*. The latter maintained a stable of gladiators, trained at his own expense, and would hire them out. At Rome it was the duty of magistrates known as *procuratores* to organise the *munera* in the name of the emperor, whose gladiators were recruited from a regular supply of prisoners of war and condemned criminals. At a show attended by the emperor it was the dubious privilege of the contestants to address him before the fighting began with the greeting: 'Ave Imperator, morituri te salutant' (Hail Emperor, those who are about to die salute you).

The whole proceedings began with a grand parade, the gladiators dressed in gold and purple robes riding in chariots to the arena. Music was provided by a variety of brass and wind instruments and by a hydraulic organ.

The combatants were paired by lot and armed according to their respective categories. For example, a *retiarius* carried a net and a trident, while a Samnite carried a large oblong shield (*scutum*), a sword (*gladius*) or spear (*hasta*), and was protected by a visored helmet, a greave on the right leg and a protective sleeve on the right arm.

The fight was to the death. When a victim fell dead or was fatally wounded he was approached by an official disguised as Charon, the ferryman of the Underworld. The latter carried a wooden mallet and struck the unfortunate individual on the head. If the loser fell exhausted or only slightly wounded, then an

73 (*below*) Music in the Roman amphitheatre: a man playing the water-organ and another with a bronze horn (*cornu*). Drawing of a Roman mosaic from Nennig, near Trier in Germany, 2nd century AD.

74 View of the interior of the Colosseum in Rome, showing the underground chambers.

75 Marble relief commemorating the release from service of two female gladiators, Amazon and Achillia. Greek, 1st or 2nd century AD.

76 (*far right*) Terracotta lamp showing two gladiators, one fallen. Roman, made in Italy *c.*15 BC–AD 15.

77 A discharge certificate issued to a gladiator released from service. His name was Moderatus, and that of his owner Lucceius. The ticket was issued on the 5th of October in the year 88.

75-77 appeal could be made to the emperor for mercy. The emperor would usually make his decision on the basis of what the crowd wished. His verdict was signalled with either an extended or a down-turned thumb.

Gladiatorial combat, although gruesome enough, was by no means the most brutal aspect of the *munera*. We hear, for example, of pairs of condemned criminals being driven into the arena, one armed and the other dressed only in a tunic. When, inevitably, the first had killed the second, the 'victor' was disarmed to become the victim of a new opponent, who was armed as he had been. Animals, too, provided the means for various forms of butchery. Wild beasts, enraged to distraction, were matched against each other in a fight to the death. Alternatively, mock hunts were set up, in which huge numbers of exotic beasts were cruelly slaughtered by so-called *bestiarii*. During the *munera* held by Titus to celebrate the inauguration of the Colosseum, no less than 5,000 wild beasts were slaughtered in a single day.

We may justifiably feel revolted by such wanton acts of cruelty and express our bewilderment at the Roman desire to gape at it. All the more disturbing is the fact that, although there were some dissenting voices among Stoic philosophers and, later, Christian moralists, the amphitheatre appears to have been attended by men and women from all levels of society. It was not only the common rabble who found pleasure in such spectacles for they were also attended and apparently enjoyed by men of taste and letters.

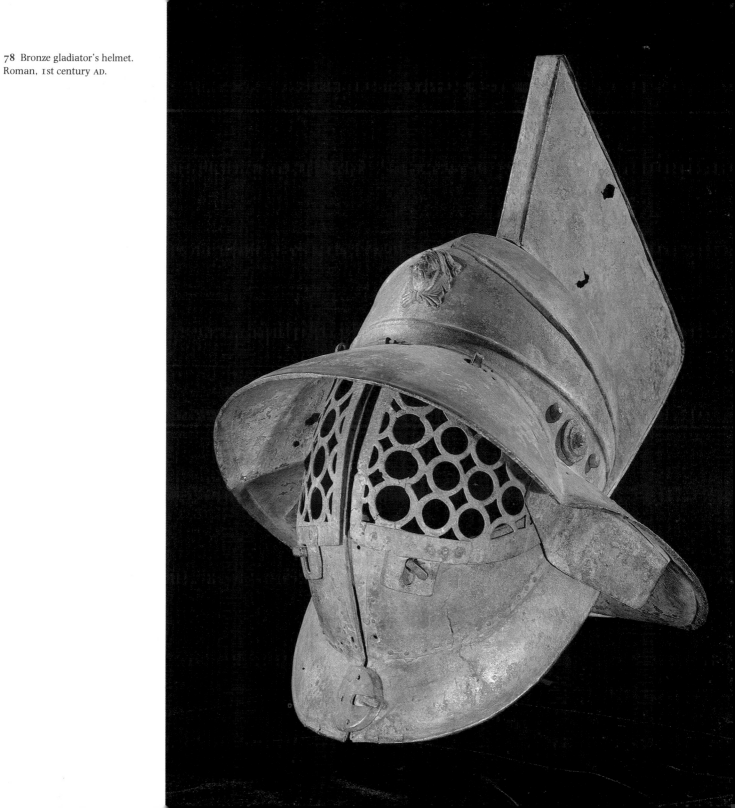

78 Bronze gladiator's helmet. Roman, 1st century AD.

8 Work and Slavery

79 Marble tombstone of an Athenian physician called Jason. He is shown seated on a stool examining the swollen belly of a child. The object on the right is a cupping-vessel shown on a much exaggerated scale. Greek, 2nd century AD.

Festivals provided a means of communication between god and man. The myth of Prometheus, as told by the early Greek poet Hesiod, explains how the divine and mortal realms were first separated and how, consequently, the need for work first arose. Zeus, father of the gods, sought to punish mankind for a crime committed against him by Prometheus, and so concealed the secret of fire. Undeterred, Prometheus, who was noted for his cunning, stole it back, hiding it in a fennel stalk. Once again Zeus took his revenge. He made the human race pay for fire by tricking them into accepting something less desirable, which the poet describes as a 'beautiful evil' (*kalon kakon*), namely woman. Hesiod describes how Hephaistos, the smith-god, 'modelled the likeness of a shy maiden out of clay' and with the help of Athena dressed his creation. The first woman was Pandora, and she it was who took the lid off the jar (which we now call Pandora's box) and unleashed all those things that were designed to afflict mankind: 'Only Hope remained there in an unbreakable home within under the rim of the great jar, and did not fly out the door.' Hitherto men had lived free from toil and they had been fed by the Earth's natural abundance. With Pandora the spell of eternal happiness was broken for ever. The secret of life was lost, and men who had once shared in the immortal gods' own immunity from pain and toil would henceforth work, suffer and die.

This story from Greek mythology illustrates a fundamental premise in the ancient attitude to work, namely that it was something done not out of choice, but out of necessity. The ancients never developed anything like the Protestant work ethic. Work was merely a means to an end, never an end in itself, and if that same end could be achieved without work, then so much the better. The precondition of a civilised life, according to the Greek philosopher Aristotle, was leisure, for it was

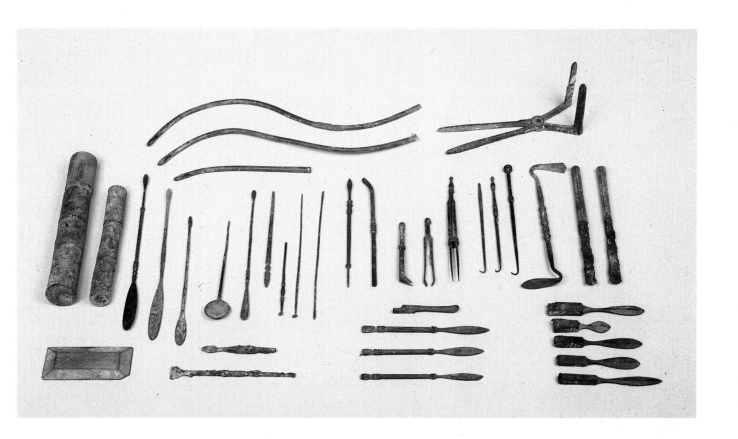

80 A set of surgical instruments and accessories including catheters, a rectal speculum, instrument cases, spatulae, scoops, probes, hooks, forceps, traction hooks and bone chisels. Roman, 1st century AD.

this that gave men the opportunity to enjoy the nobler pursuits of life. The compulsion to work could therefore be regarded as not only socially but also morally degrading. Even doctors and teachers who offered their services for hire were afforded nothing like the status they have today.

For those who were under this compulsion there existed a hierarchy of tasks, some of which were more respectable than others. The manufacturing and commercial trades were most looked down upon, while the occupation 81-84 most respected was that of farmer. The great majority of Athenians in the fifth century BC are thought to have earned their living by farming, whether as smallholders or as wealthy landowners. The original inhabitants

of Rome had also been reared on the land. From the end of the third century BC onwards, however, the sudden influx of cheap slave labour and the growth of abnormally large estates in Roman Italy dispossessed many smallholders and tenant-farmers and sent them to swell the ranks of an ever-increasing urban population.

Even in Athens, however, not everybody could be a farmer, and many made a living through manufacture and commerce. These activities were concentrated in an area of the town known as the *agora*, this being the commercial as well as the social and judicial heart of the city. All along the south and west sides of the *agora* archaeologists have found evidence of a variety of crafts, including pot-

81 A sealstone showing a shepherd and his dog. Probably Roman.

82 Terracotta lamp showing Tityrus, a character in the first *Eclogue* of the Latin poet Vergil, watching over two sheep and two goats. Roman, made in Italy *c.*AD 30–70.

83 (*left*) Black-figured *amphora* showing an olive harvest. Two bearded men beat the tree with long poles, while a youth crouches to gather the fallen fruit into a basket. A second youth has climbed the tree to beat the topmost branches with a short stick. Made in Athens *c*.520 BC. Attributed to the Antimenes Painter.

84 (*above*) Iron agricultural tools: a sickle with a tang for a wooden handle, part of a pair of shears, a pick-axe and a bill-hook.

85 Metal-working at a shaft-furnace. The man on the left appears to be removing a piece of heated metal from the furnace prior to shaping it on an anvil. The youth on the right waits with a hammer. Scene from a black-figured *oinochoe* (wine jug) made in Athens *c*.510–500 BC.

ting, bronze-working, marble-working and 85 the manufacture of terracotta figurines. The potters had their quarter in a district where the principal cemetery of the city lay, known as the Kerameikos. The black- and red-figured wares produced in the Kerameikos workshops were exported all over the Mediterranean. Athenian pottery is remarkable not only for its fine quality but also for its painted scenes of Greek mythology and daily life.

Besides farming and the manufacturing industries, the sea provided a natural source of livelihood. The Greeks were great sailors, and 87–90 both Athens and Rome became imperial powers on the strength of their navies. Neither city was self-sufficient in foodstuffs, and each relied heavily upon imports of grain from the region around the Black Sea and from Egypt. The sea, moreover, yielded its own harvest of fish, a staple of every man's diet.

The idea that all men are born equal was unthinkable in the ancient world. Fifth-century Athens is remembered as the world's first democracy, in as much as all citizens, rich and poor alike, had a say in government. The citizen body, however, excluded all women, all foreigners resident in the city and all slaves or ex-slaves. Aristotle, who was an inveterate snob and is not, therefore, always to be relied upon to represent the general view, would nevertheless have found general agreement when he argued that it was a law of nature that the free should rule over the slave, and the male over the female. Slaves were slavish by nature, and this view was shared by both Greeks and Romans. By virtue of being slaves, they were denied those moral qualities enjoyed by the free and, in particular, the well-to-do. Accordingly, the slave could be categorised along with domestic animals, with little regard for his human feelings.

If called upon to be a witness in a court of law the slave was liable to be tortured to test the truth of his evidence, and in Roman law, if a master were murdered, all those slaves who were within earshot at the time, whether implicated in the crime or not, were put to death. Further cruelties were practised on runaway slaves, and the potential runaway was branded on the face. Constantine, the first Christian emperor, ordained that this was wrong; not, however, on any humanitarian grounds but because the face was inviolate, in as much as it reflected the image of God. He decreed, therefore, that the slave should be branded on the arms and legs instead. Not even the early Christians challenged the institution of slavery or questioned the right of one man to enslave another.

People became slaves because they were the children of slaves, were captured in war or were exposed as babies and reared to slavery, or in Rome because they were convicted criminals condemned to hard labour. From around 200 BC onwards, there was a vast influx of slaves into Italy from Rome's conquests in Greece, Asia Minor, Africa and the western provinces of Gaul, Germany and Spain. Many were put to work on the land, where they were at the mercy of the bailiffs who managed the great estates of the Roman landowning aristocracy. There was probably no lot more wretched, however, than that of the mining slave, a fact which even the ancients recognised with a degree of compassion, as is illustrated by this passage from the writings of Diodorus Siculus, a Roman historian of the first century BC:

The men engaged in these mining operations produce unbelievably large revenues for their masters, but as a result of their underground excavations day and night they become physical wrecks, and because of their extremely bad conditions, the mortality rate is high; they are not allowed to give up working or have a rest, but are forced by the beatings of their supervisors to stay at their places and throw away their wretched lives as a result of these horrible hardships. Some of them survive to endure their misery for a long time because of their physical stamina or sheer will-power; but because of the extent of their suffering, they prefer dying to surviving.

The slave who fared best was one whose duties were within the family of the household to which he or she belonged. Genuine affection might grow up between a master and his trusted servant. Strong bonds could link a mistress, for example, to her childhood nurse, or a master to his one-time *paidagogos*. Household slaves under the patronage and protection of a well-to-do family might even consider themselves better off than the free but impoverished peasant.

Certainly it was not always the case that the life of a slave was one of unmitigated misery

86 Tombstone of a joiner called P. Beitenos Hermes, showing the tools of his trade. Greek, 1st or 2nd century AD. Paris, Louvre.

87 The crew of a pirate galley prepare to board a merchantman. Scene from a black-figured *kylix* (drinking cup) made in Athens *c*.520–500 BC.

88 Marble relief showing a man sailing a *corbita* (a small coastal vessel with two masts). Probably made in Africa Proconsularis (Tunisia) *c*.AD 200.

under the overseer's lash. In Athens in the second half of the fifth century BC there was even a slave police force. In Rome, during the Empire, slaves rose to positions of power at all levels of government. Many took advantage of their situation and made enough money to buy their freedom. On the whole, opportunities for manumission were greater in Rome than in Greece, and while in Athens manumitted slaves took on the status of a 'metic', or resident foreigner, and were rarely given citizenship, in Rome freedmen acquired a restricted citizen status. Indeed, they became a powerful force in Roman society, often using the entrepreneurial skills they acquired as slaves to amass vast fortunes. Here is Petronius describing the rise from rags to riches of the parvenu freedman Trimalchio in his novel *Satyricon*:

I too used to be just what you are, but I have risen as far as this by my own merits [*virtute mea*]. What men need is initiative, none of the rest matters. I buy well, I sell well; let others give you different advice. . . . Well, as I was about to say, it was thrift that brought me this good fortune. When I arrived here from Asia, I was just as big as this candlestick. Actually I used to measure my height against it day by day, and I used to anoint my lips from the lamp to get a beard on my face faster. Well, I was my owner's particular pet for fourteen years; there's nothing dishonourable in doing what your master orders. And I used to do my mistress's will too – you know what I mean: I won't spell it out, since I'm not the one to boast. But in accordance with the will of the gods, I became the master of the household, and took command of my master's little brain. And then? He nominated me co-heir with the Emperor, and I inherited an estate big enough for a senator.

Even in Rome, however, the freedman was rarely absolutely free of obligation, and it was usual for ex-slaves to be bound to their master by a form of contract through which they guaranteed to pay tribute or to provide certain services.

89 Terracotta lamp showing a fishing scene, probably in the harbour of Carthage. Made in Africa Proconsularis (Tunisia) by the lampmaker Augendus *c.*AD 200.

90 Red-figured 'fish-plate' decorated with a red mullet, a bass, a torpedo, a sargus (a sea-fish popular in Roman times but unknown today) and a cuttlefish. Made in Campania, southern Italy, *c.*350–300 BC.

F. 267

The idea of slavery is repulsive to those who have been reared on the belief that all men are born free. We must judge the ancients in their own terms, however, and not by the moral standards of our own day. There was a strong tendency among nineteenth-century scholars to idealise the Greeks, in particular, and to gloss over the essential differences between 'us' and 'them'. Towards the end of that century, in keeping with a growing interest in anthropology, scholars came to realise that even the enlightened Greeks, those lovers of democracy, builders of the Parthenon and founders of modern philosophy, had their darker side. The study of ancient religion, in particular, revealed irrational and superstitious elements in the Greek mind which, it was soon recognised, were an integral part of the Greek way of life.

The establishment of the first exhibition of Greek and Roman life at the British Museum in 1908, with its particular focus then, as now, on domestic life, may be seen historically as part of this development in Classical scholarship. Although it has gone through a number of changes, the purpose of the exhibition has always remained the same: to bring together in one room a number of objects, of interest not so much for their artistic merit as for the light they shed on the lives of the people who made and used them. It is this human interest which makes the Life Room one of the most popular and enduring of the permanent galleries at the British Museum.

91 Wooden waterwheel for draining a mine. The wheel was one of a series whose purpose was to keep the mine dry by scooping up water and carrying it up to a higher level. The wheels, arranged in pairs in vertical sequence, were each worked by a slave as a treadmill. Roman, from the Rio Tinto copper mines, Spain, 1st or 2nd century AD.

92 Bronze slave-tag. The inscription reads: 'Hold me, lest I flee, and return me to my master Viventius on the estate of Callistus' (probably in Rome). Roman, 4th century AD.

Further reading

A.B. Abrahams, *Greek Dress* (London 1908)

J.P.V.D. Balsdon, *Roman Women* (London 1962)

A.G. Beck, *Album of Greek Education* (Sydney 1975)

A. Boëthius and J.B. Ward-Perkins, *Etruscan and Roman Architecture* (Harmondsworth 1970)

S.F. Bonner, *Education in Ancient Rome* (London 1977)

A. Burford, *Craftsmen in Greek and Roman Society* (London 1972)

J. Carcopino, *Daily Life in Ancient Rome* (London 1941)

R. Flacelière, *Daily Life in Greece* (London 1965)

R.F. Forbes, *Studies in Ancient Technology*, Vol. IV, *Textiles* (London 1956)

R. Garland, *The Greek Way of Death* (London 1985)

M. Grant, *Gladiators* (London 1967)

H.A. Harris, *Sport in Greece and Rome* (London 1972)

M. Hoffmann, *The Warp-weighted Loom* (Oslo-Bergen 1965)

W.K. Lacey, *The Family in Classical Greece* (London 1968)

L.B. Lawler, *The Dance in Ancient Greece* (London 1964)

A.G. McKay, *Houses, Villas and Palaces in the Roman World* (London 1975)

A. Pickard-Campridge, *The Dramatic Festivals of Athens* (2nd ed., Oxford 1968)

H.H. Scullard, *Festivals and Ceremonies of the Roman Republic* (London 1981)

E. Simon, *Festivals of Attica* (Wisconsin 1983)

J.M.C. Toynbee, *Death and Burial in the Roman World* (London 1971)

J. Ward-Perkins and A. Claridge, *Pompeii AD 79. Catalogue to the Exhibition* (Bristol 1976)

K.D. White, *Roman Farming* (London 1970)

T. Wiedemann, *Greek and Roman Slavery* (London 1981)

L.M. Wilson, *The Clothing of Ancient Romans* (Baltimore 1938)

R.P. Winnington-Ingram, article on 'Greek Music' in *Grove's Dictionary of Music and Musicians* (London 1954, new ed. 1981)

Out of a vast periodical literature, the author has made particular use of the following:

H. Granger-Taylor, 'Weaving Clothes to Shape in the Ancient World: The Tunic and Toga of the Arringatore', *Textile History* 13 (1982), 3–25

I. Jenkins, 'Is there Life after Marriage? A Study of the Abduction Motif in Vase Paintings of the Athenian Wedding Ceremony', *Bulletin of the Institute of Classical Studies* 30 (1983), 137–45

I. Jenkins and D. Williams, 'Sprang Hair Nets: Their Manufacture and Use in Ancient Greece', *American Journal of Archaeology* 89 (1985), 411–18

J.E. Jones *et al.*, 'An Attic Country House below the Cave of Pan at Vari', *Annual of the British School of Athens* 68 (1973), 355–452

J.P. Gould, 'Law, Custom and Myth: Aspects of the Social Position of Women in Classical Athens', *The Journal of Hellenic Studies* 100 (1980), 38–59

Passages quoted from ancient authors

Page 16: Cornelius Nepos, Preface to his *Lives of Distinguished Generals*; Plutarch, *Life of Pompey*, 55.1–2 (Loeb translation). Page 27: Lucian, *Amores*, 39. Page 30: Aeschylus, *Choephoroi*, 750–63 (trans. Vellacott). Page 35: Plutarch, *Life of Lycurgus*, 16.3 (Loeb translation). Page 40: ibid., 15.3–4. Page 62: Hesiod, *Works and Days*, 96–8 (Loeb translation). Page 66: Diodorus Siculus, 5.38.1 (trans. Wiedemann). Page 68: Petronius, *Satyricon*, 75–6.

Photo acknowledgements

National Museum of Antiquities, Leiden: fig. 6; Peter Connolly: fig. 7, © Scala, Florence: fig. 8; Archaeological Museum, Naples: fig. 11; Tloopas Takis: fig. 17; Hermitage, Leningrad: fig. 18; © all rights reserved The Metropolitan Museum of Art, New York: figs 20 (Fletcher Fund, 1931), 46 (Walter C. Baker Gift, purchased 1951) and 59 (Fletcher Fund, 1956); National Museum of Finland, Helsinki: fig. 23; Deutsches Archaeologisches Institut, Rome: fig. 27; Rheinisches Landesmuseum, Trier: fig. 33; American School, Athens: fig. 38; Réunion des musées nationaux, Paris: figs 42, 86; Mansell Collection: fig. 52; Michael Holford: fig. 64, inside back cover; National Tourist Organisation of Greece: fig. 66; Robert Harding Picture Library: fig. 74.

British Museum registration and catalogue numbers of objects illustrated

Numbers are given in the order in which objects are described in the picture captions.

Front cover
GR 1966. 3–28. 22; BM Cat. Terracottas 234
Back cover
BM Cat. Silver Plate 55
Inside front cover
GR 1888.9–20.72–8; 1906.10–22.5, 1870.11–12.1, BM Cat. Bronzes 2680; British Library no. 356; GR 1906.10–22.18, 1900.6–11.4, 1893.11–2.1, 1968.2–12.1
Title page
BM Cat. Terracottas D627
Contents page
BM Cat. Vases D11

Fig
4 BM Cat. Bronzes 1574; 1584; GR 1899.2–18.46; BM Cat. Bronzes 1908
12 BM Cat. Terracottas 236
13 BM Cat. Vases E68
14 (a) BM Cat. Vases E767; (b) E453; (c) E267; (d) E508; (e) E486; (f) E49; (g) GR 1864.10–7.1522; (h) 1864.10–7.327; (i) 1978.3–17.4; (j) 1878.10–12.24, 1868.6–6.4; (k) 1756.1–1.816, 1978.1–21.34; (l) 1856.12–26.137, 1836.2–24.310
15 BM Cat. Vases B333
16 BM Cat. Vases B333
16 BM Cat. Vases B136.12–26.929; 1814.7–4.712; BM Cat. Roman Pottery, M2772; BM Cat. Bronzes 2463; GR 1856.12–26.1008; 1856.12–26.699
19 GR 1877.12–7.14; BM Cat. Silver 125; GR 1909.5–20.2; 1907.12–1.647; 1976.12–10.1; 1927.11–15.23
22 BM Cat. Vases D13
24 GR 1927.4–12.6–7
29 BM Vases GR 1905.11–2.3
30 BM Cat. Sculpture 2006
31 BM Cat. Terracottas 1655–6
32 GR 1868.1–10.359, 1881.7–9.13; 1868.5–1.75; 1906.3–10.2; 1869.2–5.6; 1931.3–18.1;

1904.2–14.1168
34 BM Cat. Vases E219
35 GR 1875.3–9.31; BM Cat. Terracottas 973; BM Cat. Vases F596; E549; GR 1926.4–19.4
36 GR 1859.3–1.48, 1873.8–20.647, 1814.7–4.1083; 1772.3–11.176, 1976.10–4.3, 1814.7–4.1091; 1905.10–21.25, 1976.11–2.3, 1907.1–19.38; 1772.3–11.250, BM Cat. Gems 3997, GR 1814.7–4.1008; 1980.4–1.2, 1980.4–1.1; 1851.8–13.333; 1974.10–9.96, 1772.3–11.80, 1772.3–11.61, 1814.7–4.1084
37 BM Vases GR 1910.6–15.4
39 BM Cat. Vases E396
40 BM Cat. Sculpture 1936
41 BM Cat. Vases B205
43 BM Cat. Terracottas 702–6
44 BM Cat. Vases E171
45 GR 1920.12–21.1
47 BM Cat. Rings 276
48 BM Cat. Sculpture 2307
49 BM Cat. Vases D62, D61, D73
50 GR 1930.4–17.1
53 BM Cat. Bronzes 858
55 BM Cat. Vases B133
56 BM Cat. Vases B134
57 BM Cat. Bronzes 2455
58 BM Cat. Vases E271
60 BM Cat. Vases E270
62 GR 1816.6–10.502
63 BM Cat. Vases E270
65 BM Cat. Vases B36
67 BM Cat. Vases 509
68 BM Cat. Terracottas 743
69 BM Cat. Vases F151
70 GR 1907.5–18.8–10
72 BM Cat. Lamps Q1349
75 BM Cat. Sculpture 1117
76 BM Cat. Lamps Q761
77 BM 1889.5–20.1
78 BM Cat. Vases 1946.5–14.1
79 BM Cat. Sculpture 629
80 GR 1968.6–26.1–39
81 BM Cat. Gems 2249
82 BM Cat. Lamps Q869
83 BM Cat. Vases B226
84 GR 1975.11–7.1; 1870.3–20.68; 1975.11–7.4; 1975.11–7.2
85 BM Cat. Vases B507
87 BM Cat. Vases B436
88 GR 1850.3–4.32

CANBY PUBLIC LIBRARY
292 N. HOLLY
CANBY, OR 97013

89 *BM Cat. Lamps* 527
90 *BM Cat. Vases* F267
91 GR 1889.6–22.1
92 *BM Cat. Bronzes* 902

Index

Figure numbers appear in bold type

Academy 48
Achilles 34, 35, 36
Aegina 24
Aeschylus 16, 30
Agamemnon 16, 53
Agora 30, 63
Akrotiri 12
Alexander the Great 20–21
Amphidromia 35
Amphitheatre 55–8, **73–8**
Andron 16
Anthesteria 30
Aristophanes 48, 53, 54, **66–8**
Aristotle 62, 65
Aristoxenus 50
Aspasia 16
Astyanax 34, **41**
Athletics 35–7, 44ff, **56–7**
Atrium 6
Augustus 19, 55

Betrothal 38
Bustuarii 57

Cassandra 53
Chariot racing 55–7, **title page, 72**
Charon 40, 42, 58, **49**
Children 30ff, **34–44**
Chiron 35, **69**
Chiton 24, 26, **25**
Chlamys, **25**
Choes 30, **35**, 37
Chorus 52
Cicero 48
Circus 55, 58, **71–2**
Clientes 7
Cloaca Maxima 11
Clytemnestra 16, 53
Colosseum 58, **74**
Comedy 53–4, **65–70**
Compluvium 6
Constantine 66
Cotton 21
Cubicula 6

Dance 49, 51, **65**, 67
Death 41ff, **49–52**
Demosthenes 14
Diodorus Siculus 66
Dionysus 49, 51
Doctors 63, **79–80**
Domus 6–8, **1–2**
Dowry 39–40
Drama 51ff, **63–70**

Ekkyklēma 53
Epidaurus 52, **66**
Euripides 50

Familia 15
Farmers 63, **83–4**
Fashions (dress) 23ff, **24–7**
Festivals 44ff
Fishing 65, **89–90**
Freedmen 68
Funerals 40ff, **49–52**
Furniture and Furnishings 22–3, **6**

Games 55, **54–6**
Gaming pieces 36
Gardens 8–9, **inside back cover, 7**
Gladiators 55ff, **75–8**
Grammatistes 36–7
Gymnasium 48, **57**
Gynaikonitis 16

Hadrian 27
Hair 26, **28**, 30
Hector 34
Herculaneum 5–7
Hermes Leader of Souls 40
Herodotus 23, 24
Hesiod 62
Hetairai 16, **13**
High-rise apartments 11, **9**
Himation 23, 25, **25**
Hoffmann, Marta 22
Horace 37
Houses, Roman 5–12, **1–2, 5, 9, 11**; Greek 12–14, **10**

Infanticide 33
Impluvium 6, **9**

Julius Caesar 55
Juvenal 29, 55

Katakysmata 39
Kithara 49, **59**, 61
Kitharistes 36
Klinē 6
Krypteia 36
Kynosarges 48

Lares 6, **3–4**
Lefkandi 19
Lenaia 53
Linen 20
Litterator 37
Loutrophoros 38, **50**
Lucian 27
Ludi 55, 57
Lyceum 48
Lykanthropos 36

Make-up 29, **32–3**
Manumission of slaves 68
Manus 15

Marriage 38ff
Military service 35, 48
Mining 66, **91**
Munera 57–8, 60
Music 35–6, 44, 48ff, 58, **44, 58–62**

Nemean games 45
Neoptolemos 34, **41**
Nepos, Cornelius 16
Nero 57

Oedipus 33
Oikos 15
Olympic Games 45
Orchestra 51–3
Oresteia 30, 53
Orestes 30
Ostia 11, **9**

Paidotribes 36, 46, 48
Palaistra 46, 48
Palla 25
Pallium 25
Panathenaia 44, 46, **54–6**
Pandora 62
Panhellenic Games 45–6
Partheonon Frieze 44
Paterfamilias 7, 15
Patronus 7
Penates 6, **3–4**
Peplos 24, 25, **25**
Pericles 16
Persian Wars 23
Petronius 68
Phlyax 54, **69**
Pins (dress) 23, 24, **24**
Pisistratus 23, 24
Plato 48
Plautus 55
Pliny 6
Plutarch 16, 40
Pompeii 5–9, **7–8**
Portraiture 32
Potty 30, **37–8**
Priam 34, **41**
Prometheus 62
Prothesis 42–3
Purple 21, 23
Pythian Games 45

Religion 6, 15, 44
Rite of Passage 42
Romulus and Remus 33

Sacrifice 38, 44, **53**
Sakkos 26
Salutatio 7
Santorini 12
School 35–8
Scipio 25
Sea 12, 65, **87–90**
Shepherds **back cover, 81–2**
Silk 21

Skēnē 53
Slaves 15, 26, 35, 62ff, **92**
Socrates 36, 53
Sparta 5, 32–3, 35–6, 40
Spinning and weaving 19–22, **19–23**
'Sprang' 26, **29**
Stola 26
Styx, River 40, **49**
Sublatus 35
Symposium 6, 49, **13**

Tablinum 6–7
Tacitus 25
Terence 55
Theatre 51ff, **63–70**
Thera 12
Thucydides 23
Timē 45
Titus 58, 60
Toga 23, 25, **26–7**
Toys **35**
Triclinium 6

Vergina 20
Vespasian 43
Vestibulum 6
Vitruvius 6–7

Wall painting 9, **8**
Weddings 38ff, **contents page, 45–8**
Wool 20–21
Women, role of 15ff
Work 62ff